Taking off the Mask: A Field Guide for Neurospicy Brains

Burnout, Awareness, and the Cost of Passing as Normal

Shaun E. Poland

Taking off the Mask: A Field Guide for Neurospicy Brains

ISBN: 979-8-9943731-0-1

This book is not a substitute for professional medical, psychological, or psychiatric care. I am not a licensed mental health professional, and nothing in this book should be taken as medical or clinical advice.

If you are experiencing a mental health emergency, thoughts of self-harm, or are in immediate danger, please contact local emergency services or a qualified medical professional right away.

If you need support, reach out to a trusted person, a healthcare provider, or a crisis support service in your area. This book is intended to offer perspective, language, and understanding, not diagnosis or treatment.

Dedication

For H.

The therapist who finally worked.

You learned my style instead of fighting it. You adapted instead of correcting.

You pushed me into discomfort without letting me drown in it.

You taught me what awareness really means, how much it can suck, and why it is still worth it.

This book is part of that learning.

And for Emily.

None of this has been easy, and you have carried more than your share of the weight.

You've lived through the confusion, the change, and the parts I couldn't put into words yet.

You believed me before I believed myself.

You are why I decided to get tested. You are why I kept going.

TABLE OF CONTENTS

PREFACE

I didn't set out to write a book.

I was diagnosed as autistic later in life, within the last year, and started therapy shortly after. Therapy cracked something open. Not in a tidy, inspirational way, but in a slow, uncomfortable, "why does this explain so much" way. I started noticing patterns. Questioning old stories. Realizing how much effort I had been spending just to look fine.

So I started writing.

At first, it was just for me. Notes. Essays. Articles. Attempts to understand why certain things felt harder than they seemed to be for other people, and why some coping strategies helped while others made things worse. I was trying to learn how my brain worked, not just how to tolerate it.

When I went looking for books to help, I struggled. Not because they were bad, but because they didn't work for me. Many were written in a clinical voice that felt distant, or from a neurotypical perspective that explained neurodivergence without fully inhabiting it. Others were deeply experiential but light on the "why," and my brain needed the reasoning, not just the story.

I wanted something that sat in the middle. Honest, direct, sometimes messy, but still grounded in understanding. Curious without being overly academic. Lived-in without being vague.

So I kept writing in my own style.

At some point, these pieces started to look like a book.

This book is not a comprehensive guide to autism, ADHD, or neurodivergence. It's not a diagnostic manual. I'm not a therapist, psychologist, or psychiatrist. I don't have a degree in mental health, and I'm not trying to replace professional care.

What I am offering is perspective. Language. Pattern recognition. A field guide built from lived experience, research, therapy, and a lot of trial and error.

This book was written for me. If you see yourself in it, that's a gift. If parts of it don't fit you, that's expected. Neurodivergence isn't a scale where we all land on different numbers. It's a collection of different systems, sensitivities, coping strategies, and survival skills that show up in different ways.

You're not meant to copy my experience. You're meant to adapt to what resonates.

Some chapters will hit harder than others. Some may feel obvious. Some might irritate you. That's okay. You don't have to agree with everything here for it to be useful. You don't even have to read it in order.

If you're someone who doesn't believe in autism, neurodivergence, or mental health more broadly, this book probably isn't for you. My experiences are real. I'm not interested in defending them.

What I do hope is that this book helps people be a little kinder. Kinder to themselves. Kinder to others. Especially in places where people are quietly working very hard just to look normal.

If you're late-diagnosed, self-questioning, burned out, masking, or just tired of feeling like you're doing life on hard mode without knowing why, I hope the first few chapters make you say, "Yes. That. Exactly that."

And if you're someone who loves, works with, or lives alongside a neurodivergent person, I hope this gives you a clearer picture of what you may not see from the outside.

You don't need to fix anything while reading this. You don't need to have revelations on a schedule. Just noticing is enough to start.

That's where this book begins.

How Did We Get Here?

You look fine.

Maybe even successful. Functional. "So capable." The friend people come to for advice. The coworker who "always somehow pulls it off."

Inside, you feel like you're running too hot, one bad day away from shutting down.

Welcome to the quiet burnout of looking normal.

This book is about quiet burnout and the cost of looking normal. It's also about what happens after you realize you've been living your life on hard mode, when your past suddenly makes sense, and your brain starts asking, Okay, now what?

We'll move through a few kinds of chapters together. Some are story chapters where I'll walk you through my late-diagnosis chaos so you can see how this plays out in a real, messy life, not just bullet points. Other chapters go under the hood, where we'll look at how your brain and body react to stress, including neuroplasticity, your brain's ability to change with practice and support.

Then we'll talk about what happens when you melt down, shut down, or fade away, and how those moments aren't moral failures or proof you're broken, but signs that your system hit its limit.

There are chapters that talk about therapy and awareness, not as magical fixes, but as tools you can choose from, like a field kit. And there are very practical chapters that turn all of this into small, real-world adjustments to how you plan your time, set up your environment, and talk to the people in your life. By the end, you won't have a brand-new brain, but you will have a clearer map, a kinder story about yourself, and some practical levers you can pull to make life easier.

The life you built on hard mode

If you're reading this, I'm guessing at least one of these is already true: Life has felt weirdly harder for you than it seemed to be for everyone else. School. Work. Relationships. Laundry even. Your brain has been running the advanced difficulty setting while everyone around you played the tutorial, so you handled schoolwork and social cues while also managing extra sensory or focus challenges.

On the outside, it looked like you "just pushed through." Good grades, or at least "so much potential." Decent career. People who rely on you. Maybe a partner, kids, a mortgage, a slightly underwatered plant. Your data clearly shows you can function.

Inside, though, you have data that screams, "this has always felt like too much."

Both are true.

You may have only recently discovered words like ADHD, autism, or even AuDHD, and watched your entire history rearrange itself in your head. ADHD might mean your focus, time management, and impulse control have been playing on expert mode this whole time. Autism might mean noticing that your brain has been processing the world and social rules on a different channel. AuDHD is a term people use when traits of both autism and ADHD show up together, which can look like big sensory reactions and trouble with focus or time management happening all at the same time.

You didn't decide to run your life this way. You were just born with a brain that notices more, feels more, jumps more, and freezes more. You grew up in a world that kept handing you neurotypical instruction manuals, written for the kind of brains the culture treats as the default. Then you find yourself stuck staring at that invisible manual and saying, “Let's get this over with.”

So you did things like forcing yourself to make eye contact in class even when it burned, laughing along at loud lunch tables even though the noise made your skin buzz, or copying the way other people talk so you wouldn't sound “weird.”

You got very, very good at looking normal.

And it's been exhausting.

Late diagnosis and that “am I starting over?” feeling

Finding out you might be neurodivergent in your late 20s, 30s, 40s, or even beyond is like someone quietly sliding a user manual across the table after you've already built the entire IKEA bedroom set. With no tools. In the dark.

Part of you feels relieved: Suddenly, the constant fatigue, the strange social rules, the weird relationship with time, and the way your brain ricochets between hyperfocus and “I cannot remember my own name or phone number” actually make sense. You weren’t lazy or flaky or dramatic. Your brain was just trying to run a very intense operating system without the proper support.

Another part of you feels furious: Where was this information in middle school, when you were crying over homework that took you five hours and your friends thirty minutes? Where was it in your first job, when you thought everyone else actually could answer emails, do deep work, and socialize at lunch without needing to hide in a bathroom stall and stare at the wall?

And then there is that quiet panic... Am I supposed to start over now?

New habits, new coping skills, new boundaries, new everything. It can feel like you've been living in a house that is technically standing but secretly held together with duct tape and bungee cords. Now someone is telling you, “Good news, you can actually fix the wiring.” And your nervous system is like, “I can’t even fix my kitchen drawer.”

If that's you, you're not alone. You're also not late. You're right on time for the information you have.

You're not starting from zero. You're starting from experienced, tired, and finally informed.

The quiet burnout no one saw

We talk a lot about burnout when it looks like a collapse. You can’t work. You can’t get out of bed. Your brain has gone offline. But there's another kind of burnout that hides in plain sight.

It looks like: You still show up. You still get it done. You still smile. You still remember birthdays, hit deadlines by the skin of your teeth, and even crack jokes in meetings.

You also forget simple words. You stare at your phone and cannot process a text. You feel like you live at level 7 out of 10 on the overwhelm dial, with occasional spikes to 12. Your body never quite turns off, even when you're lying on the couch “resting.”

You might think, “I can’t be burnt out. I’m still functioning.”

That is the trap.

Quiet burnout is what happens when you have spent years or even decades using your entire brain just to hit "average." You trained yourself to read every room, second-guess every reaction, and pre-plan every conversation. You built a full-time job out of masking and called it "being good with people."

You might have sharpened your emotional IQ to survive. You learned to read tiny changes in tone, micro-expressions, and patterns in how people behave. You turned it into a skill. Maybe even a career advantage. People might say you are "so intuitive" or "so emotionally intelligent."

They don't see that your intuition is basically a high-powered pattern-recognition engine that never sleeps. It watches everything, all the time, trying to keep you safe from rejection, conflict, embarrassment, or that feeling of "I got it wrong again."

It's like having six extra tabs of reality open. Background noise that never quite goes silent.

No wonder you are tired.

"Looking normal" as a full-time job

When you grow up neurodivergent without knowing it, you get very good at masking.

Masking is all the tiny, constant adjustments you make so other people feel comfortable, and you don't get labeled as "too much," "too weird," or "too intense."

You notice how long other people make eye contact, so you copy that. You mirror their posture. You study how your coworkers chat about weekends, so you build a little script of acceptable answers. You laugh when others laugh, even if you didn't actually find it funny, because you are tracking the rules, not the joke.

You might even praise yourself for it. "See, I'm great at reading people. I'm adaptable. I can fit in anywhere."

What you're really saying is, "I am spending a massive amount of mental energy to run an invisible social translator in the background at all times."

That translator costs something. Usually, it costs you.

By the time you get home, your words are gone. Your patience is gone. Your ability to decide what to eat is gone. You have been high-effort normal for eight or nine or ten hours, and now your brain is like, "We are done. Goodbye."

So you scroll. Or you drink. Or you doomshop. Or you hyperfixate on some tiny corner of the internet that feels like breathing. You do whatever helps your brain come back down from the day's performance.

From the outside, again, you look fine.

On the inside, it is a quiet, ongoing burnout.

What this book is (and what it is not)

This book is not a medical textbook. It will not replace a doctor, a therapist, or an official diagnosis. It will not tell you "every person with ADHD or autism is like this."

This is a field guide from inside the experience. It's stitched together from years of over-researching, therapy sessions, and trial-and-error experiments I originally ran just to keep myself afloat, and now I'm handing you the version I wish I'd had decades ago.

I am writing for the part of you that is half "holy shit, that's me" and half "what do I even do with this information?"

We're going to talk about things like:

- Work, and why your brain rebels the second someone puts a time sheet near it
- Alcohol and other "numbing hacks" that sneak in when you are always on high alert
- Relationships, and what happens when your emotional IQ is sky-high but your nervous system is fried
- Masking, unmasking, and the weird in-between, where you're not sure who you are without the performance

Each chapter is its own little ecosystem. You can absolutely read this book from start to finish. There is a lot of context that will help things click together if you do. You can also skip around. If work is burning you out, start there. If you are mostly wrestling with friendships, marriage, or dating, jump to that. If you are just here for the "why am I like this" neuroscience, you can hang out with those bits first and circle back later.

This book grew out of individual pieces I wrote over time, so there will be some overlap, a bit of repetition, and the occasional idea that shows up more than once from a slightly different angle. I have done my best to keep the transitions clean and the topics flowing, but my ADHD brain also put things in the order that made the most sense to me.

Your attention, your energy, and your curiosity are not problems to fix. They are navigation tools. Use them.

You are not broken, you are overloaded

One of the most important things I want you to hear, before we go any further, is this: You are not broken for finding life hard.

You have been doing life with a nervous system tuned differently, in a world built for other settings. You can love your brain, appreciate your creativity, your pattern-spotting, your sensitivity, and still be very, very tired from how much effort it has taken to pass for "fine."

Both are true.

You're allowed to feel relieved, furious, sad, hopeful, and curious, all in the same 10-minute period. You're allowed to grieve the years you spent thinking it was a personal failing, and you're allowed to look back at your life like a detective, collecting clues you missed the first time through.

You're also allowed to want more than just "not burnt out." You get to want a life where your brain is not running in hard mode all the time, where you're not constantly shape-shifting to be acceptable, where rest is not something you earn with suffering.

We're going to talk about practical things, tiny experiments, and gentle shifts that start to make that possible. We're going to name what has been invisible. We're going to unpick the tangle between "this is my personality" and "this is a survival skill I built under pressure."

You don't have to figure everything out at once. Unfortunately, you most likely won't, as much as you want to. And that's okay.

For now, it is enough that you're here, reading this, letting it land.

If some part of you is already whispering, "Wait. That explains so much," then good.

That is the part I've been writing this for.

Next, I will ground these ideas in my personal story of a late diagnosis so you can see what it looks like in everyday life.

Too Weird for "Normal," Too Normal for "Autistic": A Late Diagnosis Story

In the last chapter, we talked about you, the tired transformer who looks "fine" on the outside. Before we dig deeper into your patterns, I want to show you how this has played out in one very specific life: mine. I was 39 when someone finally named what I had been living with, autism.

On paper, that seemed simple. In reality, it was a ten-year slow burn. It began when my girlfriend, now my wife, asked me from the other side of the car whether I might be autistic. She used the word Asperger syndrome, a term some people still use, though today most clinicians describe those traits as part of autism.

I had not.

We talked about what she meant. She mentioned the social stuff, the intense focus, and how I melted down over changes others treated like speed bumps. As we Googled and analyzed the symptoms, something in my brain quietly clicked into place. Not a complete puzzle, but more like the feeling you get when you find a piece that probably belongs in that cluster you have been staring at for hours.

Then I did what many adults do.

I shrugged it off.

Autism, I thought, is something doctors spot in kids. I was an adult and already had a bag full of labels. I was diagnosed with depression and anxiety when I was younger, and both still hit me in waves. ADHD was diagnosed later in life, and made focus and follow-through harder than it was for other people. And I was diagnosed with OCD a few years back, in my mid-30s, which made my thoughts stick. I didn't exactly feel eager to add another label or acronym to the collection. So I told myself, "Interesting theory," and then I tucked it back into the part of my brain where things go to die.

Fast forward four or five years. My career continued advancing into more senior roles. The expectations increased. The meetings got longer. The office politics, meaning the unspoken rules and power games at work, got more complex. And underneath all that, something in me started to fray.

Burnout is the polite word.

What it felt like was dragging myself through every day in wet cement. It felt like knowing exactly what I needed in order to function, while also feeling embarrassed and guilty for needing those things in the first place. It felt like being too tired to keep pretending I was fine.

For a long time, I tried to hide it. I already felt like I had enough on my plate. I didn't want one more label. I told myself I should be able to push through, to cope better, to try harder. You might know that script. A lot of us do.

Eventually, I did something new.

I told my doctor I wanted a referral for autism testing.

That is the short version of how I arrived here, writing this, trying to explain what the autism spectrum feels like from the inside. Not as a straight line that runs from “not autistic” to “very autistic,” but as something more complex, more accurate, and honestly, more human. Imagine a soundboard with lots of sliders, each one a different trait, like sensory sensitivity, social energy, need for routine, or how fast your brain jumps. Your pattern isn't a single point on a line. It's the shape all those sliders make together.

If you walk away from this with one core idea, I hope it's this: The autism spectrum is not a single slider. It is a whole mixing board.

The problem with the "more or less autistic" idea

You know the way people say things like, "He's autistic, but you would never know," or "She doesn't speak much, so she must be more autistic." Maybe someone has even joked, "We're all a little autistic, right?" But autism isn't a quirky personality label. It's a real neurotype that shapes how a person senses, communicates, and recovers from stress. Those comments are doing something in your head, even if no one sits you down and explains it.

Most people have absorbed a simple mental picture of autism. Even if no one ever drew it out, you probably have something like this in your head.

At one end, there is “mild,” or “high functioning.” At the other end, “severe,” or “low functioning.” People imagine all autistic folks lined up somewhere along that line, like a volume knob that you can turn up or down.

More autistic. Less autistic.

That model isn't just inaccurate. It's lazy.

It makes it sound like we are all the same kind of person, just with different amounts of autism poured in. It turns a rich, varied set of brains into a single ranking system. And it quietly encourages people to treat some autistic folks as "basically normal" and others as "too far gone," which is painful and wrong in more ways than I can fit into one book.

It also does something sneaky.

It trains you to assume you understand someone just because you know they're autistic. Or just because you know one other autistic person.

You meet an autistic coworker who is very verbal and good in meetings, and your brain file labeled "autism" updates to, "Oh, so it is mostly a social awkwardness thing." You meet a nonverbal autistic adult who uses an AAC device, and your file updates to, "Oh, so it is mostly a can't live independently thing." Every new person gets squeezed into the same one-dimensional line.

If you're autistic yourself, that line can turn against you. You might start asking, "Am I autistic enough?" Or, "If they can do that and I can't, does that mean I'm failing?" Or the classic, "I can pass as neurotypical most days, does that mean I'm being dramatic about this diagnosis?"

The line doesn't help anybody.

So let us throw it out and start again.

Think mixing board, not scale

Imagine an audio mixing board in a music studio, the kind with a whole row of little sliders you can push up and down, kind of like the volume and brightness sliders on your phone. Each slider controls something different. Vocals. Bass. Treble. Effects. You move each one up or down to change the way the whole song feels, and no single slider tells you whether the track is "good" or "bad." You need to look at the whole pattern.

That is much closer to how autism works.

Autistic people are not all “more or less” of the same thing. We are a collection of patterns across many different internal sliders. Some of my sliders are turned way up. Some are in the middle. Some aren't very different from the average person at all.

Two people can both be autistic, both very much so, and still look completely different from each other because their sliders are set in different configurations.

This is what people mean when they talk about the spectrum being “not a line but a color wheel” or “not more or less, just different.” Those metaphors point to the same reality. There are spectrums inside the spectrum.

You can think of it like this: there is no single “autism slider” that you move up to make someone “more autistic.” There are lots of sliders that live inside what we call autism. Social processing. Sensory sensitivity. Need for routine. Ability to mask. Verbal communication. And so on.

The diagnosis doesn't tell you where every slider is set. It just tells you, “You have a mixing board like this. Some of these sliders are going to matter for you.”

The specific shape of your pattern is what makes you, you.

A few of the sliders on my board

To keep this grounded, let me show you a little bit of my own mixing board. I won't hit every slider, but here are a few that have shaped my life.

Social processing

If you meet me now, especially in a work context, you might not guess that I'm autistic.

I can hold eye contact when I need to. I understand jokes. I can run a meeting, make small talk, and even come across as confident. This is where the old "high functioning" label tends to show up, because people see those visible behaviors and think, "Oh, you must be on the mild end then."

What you don't see is the amount of processing and masking that is happening underneath.

My "social understanding" slider isn't turned quite all the way down. I do understand people. I have spent years studying them. Reading about communication. Watching every interaction like a tiny science project. I have built a big internal library of rules and scripts.

But that effort comes with a cost.

It's like running social interactions in a very detailed manual mode, rather than the automatic mode most people use. I can do it. I might even do it well. I just burn a lot more fuel per mile.

This is where the "scale" picture breaks. People see one slider, the visible behavior, and assume they know my whole setup. They don't see the internal math or the fatigue.

Sensory sensitivity

Now look at a different slider.

The sensory one, the "how loud the world feels" slider, is turned way up for me. No one needed to teach me that. My body announces it every time a light buzzes at the wrong pitch or three people try to talk over each other. Some people around me will actually notice the flicker in my right eye when this happens.

In a typical one-dimensional model, someone might say, "You seem fine socially, so you must be less autistic." But that same “fine” person might be getting knocked flat by fluorescent lights, perfume, or the sound of a vacuum cleaner.

This is where two autistic people can look like opposites from the outside. One might be very verbal but melt down from noise. Another might have limited speech but seek out lots of sensory input, spinning, jumping, and stimming happily in environments that would send me into shutdown.

Neither is “more autistic.” Their sensory sliders are just set differently.

Routine, change, and burnout

Another slider on my board is the “need for predictability.”

Change is hard for me. Not every change. I'm not frozen in time. But sudden shifts in plans, unclear expectations, or environments where “everything is urgent” all hit that slider and send an alarm through my nervous system.

For a long time, I didn't know this was an autistic thing. I thought it was a personal failing. So I did what you do when you think you're failing. I tried harder. Took on more. Learned to work in chaos. Said yes when I wanted to scream no.

That is how you end up in burnout.

In the old spectrum picture, burnout can look like “getting worse.” As if the knob moved up the scale. In the mixing board picture, burnout occurs when you keep forcing your sliders into positions that don't match your wiring. You can do it for a while. Sometimes for years. Then your system pushes back.

If you're autistic, you might recognize this. You cope, cope, cope, until one day you just can't do it anymore. Then you wonder if you have “lost” skills or gone backwards. From the inside, it feels more like your brain finally refusing to run on emergency power all the time.

Why the mixing board matters

So, why does this metaphor matter, beyond being a neat visual? Because the way you picture autism shapes the way you treat autistic people. And it shapes the way autistic people treat themselves.

If you hold the “single line” model in your head, a lot of unhelpful habits sneak in.

You start comparing one autistic person to another as if you are ranking them. You assume that strategies that work for one person “on the spectrum” should work for everyone else. You might even feel confused or suspicious when someone’s visible behavior doesn't match the stereotype you have attached to their place on the line.

You can end up saying things like:

- “You can't be that autistic, you make eye contact.”
- “My friend’s kid is autistic, and they can't do that, so you must be exaggerating.”
- “If you can work full-time, your autism must be mild.”

None of that makes sense if you think in sliders.

In the mixing board model, “eye contact” isn't a total score. It's a single slider that can be influenced by a bunch of other sliders, such as masking, anxiety, culture, learned scripts, and so on. Employment status isn't a total score either. Plenty of autistic people hold complex jobs while struggling with basic daily tasks, or the other way around.

The question stops being, "Where are you on the line?" and becomes, "What does your pattern look like, and what do you need?"

For autistic people ourselves, this shift is even more important.

The mixing board lets you say, "I'm not broken because I don't match that other autistic person's life." It lets you understand why one coping strategy feels natural, and another feels like wearing someone else's shoes. It gives you language to explain yourself that goes beyond "I'm weird, sorry."

Instead of asking whether you're "autistic enough," you can start asking much better questions, like, "Which sliders are causing me the most stress right now?" or "Where am I pushing myself to look more typical at the cost of my health?"

Those questions lead to helpful answers.

Same diagnosis, different patterns

Let us look at what this means for the people around you.

You might know two autistic coworkers. One talks a lot in meetings, sometimes too much, and misses subtle signals when people are bored. Another is quiet in groups but gives brilliant written feedback afterward. If you only think in "more or less autistic," you might assume the talkative one is "more social" and the quiet one is "more severe."

In reality, both of them might have very similar internal sliders for social cognition, but very different sliders for anxiety, sensory overwhelm, or expressive language.

You might see an autistic friend who loves parties but needs two days alone afterward. Another who avoids parties completely but can talk for three hours one-on-one. The party lover is not "less autistic" because they like people. They might have a different balance of sensory, social, and recovery sliders.

From the outside, these differences are easy to misread.

One of the most common mistakes people make is treating visible independence as a sign of being "less autistic" and visible support needs as a sign of being "more autistic." In the mixing board model, independence isn't a single slider. It's the outcome of many sliders working together, plus the environment, plus support.

Give someone the right accommodations, clear communication, and a predictable routine, and suddenly their board looks different. They might speak more. Work more. Smile more. Remove those supports, and their system starts to short out again.

The internal wiring hasn't magically changed.

The context did.

When you understand that there are spectrums inside the spectrum, you stop treating each autistic person as a walking stereotype and start treating them as an individual configuration of needs and strengths.

Which sounds basic, but if you've ever had your experience dismissed with "that's not what autism looks like," you know it's not automatic.

Why one person's "fix" might be your nightmare

There is another reason this matters.

If you hang out in autistic spaces, online or in person, you'll find a lot of advice. Some of it is life-changing. Some of it is… less so. Not because the advice is bad in itself, but because it's designed for a different configuration of sliders.

One autistic person swears by noise-cancelling headphones and loves the feeling of deep pressure, weighted blankets, tight hugs, the works. Another finds those exact same things suffocating and stressful. Both are valid. Their sensory sliders are just tuned differently.

One person might say, “Eye contact is painful, so I never do it.” Another might say, “I do eye contact as a conscious choice because it makes conversations smoother.” Both are making adjustments based on their own board. Neither is more or less autistic.

If you are newly diagnosed, this can be confusing.

You try something that helped another autistic person, and it does nothing for you. Or it makes things worse. You might start to wonder if you are doing autism wrong. You are not. You are simply discovering your sliders.

The goal isn't to copy someone else’s setup. The goal is to learn enough about your own pattern that you can experiment intelligently. To say, this part of my board looks similar to that person, so maybe their tool will help me. And this part looks very different, so their tool might not fit.

It's the difference between thinking, “All autistic people are like this,” and thinking, “All autistic people have some kind of mixing board inside of them, and I just need to learn how mine works.”

Seeing the hidden work

If you aren't autistic yourself but love or work with someone who is, the mixing board model can also help you see the hidden work they do.

Remember my social slider.

From the outside, a “high masking” autistic person might look relaxed and capable. You see the meeting, but you don't see the script preparation, the mental rehearsal, the debrief afterward, the way they replay every sentence in their head on the drive home. You don't feel their sensory system picking up every flicker of light and chair scrape.

When you know that, you stop saying things like, “You handle this so well, you must not really need accommodations,” and start saying things like, “If this looks easy, it might be because you're working very hard. What would make it genuinely easier for you?”

On the other side, a “low masking” autistic person might stim openly, ask for breaks, or use assistive tech. You might be tempted to view them as “more autistic,” when actually they're just showing you the work instead of hiding it. Their sliders might not be that different from yours. Their willingness, or need, to drop the mask is.

Once you stop treating all these differences as a hierarchy, you can start treating them as information.

Information you can use to support someone properly.

Information you can use to stop saying, “But you did this yesterday,” when someone hits a limit today. Because in mixing board terms, yesterday might have been a quiet room with lots of control, and today might be a noisy, chaotic mess that slams every slider into the red.

So what do we do with this?

If the autism spectrum is a mixing board full of sliders instead of a single line, what do we actually do with that idea?

First, we retire the “more or less autistic” language. It does more harm than good. Instead, we can talk about support needs, energy costs, or specific experiences. "He needs help with communication." "She gets overwhelmed by noise." "They mask heavily at work and crash at home."

That is more precise and more respectful.

Second, we can get more curious about individual patterns. For autistic people, that might look like noticing what drains you and what steadies you, and not judging yourself when your sliders don't match the person next to you. For non-autistic people, it might look like asking, "What part of this situation is hardest for you?" rather than assuming.

Third, we stop treating any one slider as the whole story.

An autistic person who speaks clearly is not automatically "fine." An autistic person who needs help with daily tasks is not automatically "childlike" or "less than." The mixing board reminds you that competence in one area does not erase difficulty in another, and vice versa.

Finally, we remember that exploring, talking to others, and learning more are part of this process for everyone.

You might try adjustments that do nothing. You might borrow strategies from someone whose board is totally different and realize, "Nope, that's not for me." That's not failure. That's data.

Every conversation you have, every story you read from another autistic person, is another glimpse at a different mixing board. The point isn't to copy them. The point is to realize how many valid patterns exist, and to give yourself permission to honor your own.

Not broken, just tuned differently

When my wife first asked about autism, I treated it like a side note. A theory. Interesting, but not something I allowed to change how I saw myself.

A decade later, after burnout, a diagnosis, and a lot of quiet rethinking, I see it very differently.

Being autistic doesn't mean I sit at some fixed point on a single spectrum. It means my brain is tuned in a particular, uneven way. Very high here. Very low there. Comfortable in some contexts. Absolutely wrecked in others.

It means that when I walk into a room, my mixing board comes with me.

Yours does too, whether you're autistic or not. We all have our own sliders. Autism just means some of mine sit far enough from the average that the world, as it is currently built, can be hard to live in without conscious adjustments.

If there's anything I hope you take from this, it's that autistic people are not templates that you can rank. We are configurations. Patterns. Whole boards of settings that add up to a person.

So the next time you catch yourself thinking, "He's more autistic than she is," or, "I must be less autistic because I can do X," try translating that thought. Ask instead, "Which sliders am I looking at, and which ones am I missing?"

Everything gets clearer from there.

Dear Newly Diagnosed: Awareness Is Exhausting (And You Are Still Doing It Right)

You know that moment when you're too tired to think, but your brain didn't get the memo?

You're on the couch. Your body is done. Your day is over. Your mind, however, is running a full performance review of everything you did in the last twelve hours.

What went well? What you could've done better? That thing you said that was fine. That thing you said that was maybe weird. Or maybe that thing you forgot to say, and now it's too late.

You don't want to do this. It's just happening. And you're sitting there thinking, very politely, "I would like to unsubscribe now... please."

If that sounds familiar, I want you to know something very simple and very important.

You are not failing at awareness. You are already too good at it.

When “awareness” feels like homework you didn't sign up for

If you are newly diagnosed with anything in the neurodivergent neighborhood, you've probably heard some version of:

- “Awareness is the first step.”
- “You just need to be more aware of your patterns.”
- “Once you notice it, you can change it.”

This sounds reasonable on paper. It may even sound like a lightbulb moment. You imagine a gentle inner voice that goes, "oh, I see what I'm doing there," and then your life gets 12 percent easier.

What often happens instead is closer to what you described on that couch.

You're extremely aware. You notice your tone, your body, your thoughts, your timing, the other person’s micro-expressions, the context, the history, the future consequences, and the weather.

You run through the day like a security camera replay, looking for clues. You clock every moment you were “too much,” “too blunt,” “too slow,” “too sensitive,” or just “not how people are supposed to be.”

It's not a cute little insight. It is a full-time monitoring system.

No wonder you are exhausted.

Your brain was “aware” long before anyone gave it a name

Here is the part no one tells you. This level of awareness didn't appear after you got diagnosed. It has been there the whole time. If you grew up feeling different and didn't have language for it, your brain probably built a quiet system of constant scanning to keep you safe.

You were watching:

- What made people frown
- What made them laugh
- What made them leave the room
- What made them stay

You learned to track yourself like a science experiment. You noticed which versions of you got rewarded and which versions got shut down.

That is awareness. It is just awareness that is wired for survival, not for self-kindness.

So when someone now says, "Just be more aware," it can feel like they are handing homework to the kid who already did the whole project, the extra credit, and then cried in the bathroom.

You are not starting from zero. You are starting from overdrive.

The myth of "blank mind" people

A lot of us carry this quiet fantasy that other people's brains are peaceful.

We watch someone lean back on a couch and think, their mind probably just sits there in neutral, humming softly, like a parked car.

Meanwhile, your mind is more like a busy airport. Arrivals, departures, announcements, turbulence, delayed flights, lost luggage, and a raccoon on the runway for no clear reason.

It's very easy, from inside the airport, to assume that you're doing awareness wrong. You picture that other people:

- Notice a thing
- Have a brief, wise thought about it
- Gently adjust

You, on the other hand, notice a thing, then eleven more things, then your entire life, and now you are on the couch two days later still thinking about a conversation that lasted four minutes. And what about that damn raccoon?

Here's the reframe.

Your brain is not failing. It is thorough.

It's not that other people have some perfect, calm awareness you don't have access to. It's that your awareness was trained to over-function for years, often in the dark, without support.

You are not less aware. You are heavier with it.

Awareness is not supposed to hurt this much

Let us be clear about something.

The point of awareness is not to create a 24/7 internal performance review that constantly docks you points and makes you feel like you may never catch up. The point of awareness is to give you more choice and less suffering. When awareness hurts this much, it's usually because it is doing one of these jobs:

- Acting as an internal critic, replaying the day and grading you
- Acting as a security guard, scanning for danger or rejection

- Acting as a historian, dragging in every similar moment from the past

- Acting as a fortune teller, trying to prevent anything bad in the future

That couch brain that wouldn't stop? That wasn't "you being dramatic." That was a very old system, running very old code, trying very hard to protect you.

Of course you wanted it to stop. That doesn't mean you're bad at awareness. It means your awareness is unfiltered and unsupervised.

Which brings us to the real work.

Not "more awareness."

Different awareness.

Turning the volume down, not turning yourself off

You don't actually need to get rid of awareness. You wouldn't want to. It's the part of you that notices patterns, reads rooms, remembers details, and spots trouble early.

The goal is more like adjusting a sound system.

Right now, your awareness might be like a speaker turned up to maximum, pressed against your ear. Every small sound is deafening. Every small misstep feels like a failure.

What you're allowed to do, now that you know more about your brain, is start touching the volume knob.

Not every thought gets to be a siren. Not every moment needs a full debrief. You can know, for example, "I was not at my best in that conversation" without running a 45-minute mental documentary about it. You can think, “I wish today had gone differently,” and then also think, “I am allowed to sleep now.”

This is a different kind of awareness. It notices, then it stops.

Not because you're ignoring things. But because you are allowed to be a person, not a constant self-audit.

Why you feel so tired all the damn time

Let us circle back to that two-day stretch that finally eased today.

You had:

- A full day of being a human in the world
- A whole night of involuntary mental replay
- A next day where the same process tagged along, even when you tried to get out of the house

That is a lot. Of course you're drained.

This isn't a moral failure. This is an energy problem. Awareness costs energy. Hyper-awareness costs a lot of energy. Every time your brain reviews, rewrites, predicts, or replays, it's burning through your fuel.

If no one ever told you that, it's very easy to assume that you are simply lazy or weak when you hit that wall on the couch.

You are not. You're simply running a very advanced system on a human-sized battery.

Fatigue is not proof that you're doing awareness wrong. Fatigue is proof that you've been doing too much of it, for too long, without support.

You don't have to earn rest by solving yourself

One more quiet lie that often sneaks in after diagnosis is this: "I can rest once I figure myself out."

So you sit on the couch and think, If I can just understand why I did that, if I can just make sure I do better tomorrow, then I'll feel better, and then I can finally relax.

Except the finish line keeps moving. There's always one more moment you could review, one more thing you could have said, one more angle to consider.

Here is the reframe I want to gently offer yourself: You don't need to complete a full emotional audit of your day before you're allowed to rest.

You're allowed to be unfinished. You're allowed to be mid-process. You're allowed to say, "I did what I could today, and the rest will have to wait."

That is not denial. That's boundaries within your own awareness.

It is you saying, "Thank you, brain, I know you're trying to help, but the office is closed for tonight."

You are not behind, you are overloaded

If you walk away with only one sentence, let it be this: You are not failing at awareness. You are just drowning in it.

Being newly diagnosed doesn't mean you suddenly have to become some perfect, mindful, always-self-observing version of yourself.

In fact, you might need the opposite. You might need permission to be less tuned in, less analyzed, less "on."

You are allowed to be a messy, learning human who sometimes only realizes what happened three days later. You are allowed to forget half of what your therapist said. You are allowed to say, “I actually don't want to think about this anymore right now.”

Your awareness is not a problem to fix. It is a powerful tool that has been working unsupervised for a very long time.

You are just starting to meet it on purpose.

So when you find yourself on the couch, brain sprinting through the day while your body begs for sleep, try this tiny shift.

Instead of, “Why can't I just be more aware in the right way?” Try, “Of course I'm tired. This is a lot. I'm not failing. I'm just learning where the off switch is.”

You are not behind. You are overloaded. And that is something you are absolutely allowed to do less of.

From here, we’re going to look at one of the main supports people try after a diagnosis, therapy, and how to make it work for your brain instead of turning it into one more exhausting job.

"THAT'S THE FUCKING POINT, MAN": LEARNING TO HATE THERAPY THE RIGHT WAY

Yes, this chapter title is loud on purpose. If therapy talk makes you want to flip a table or close this book, I want you to know I'm taking that reaction seriously, not trying to talk you out of it.

Once you realize your brain is wired differently, the next question usually shows up fast and loud: "Okay, so… now what?" You have this new label, this new map, and zero idea what to actually do with it on a Tuesday afternoon when your inbox is eating you alive. For a lot of us, that is the moment someone says, "You should probably talk to a therapist," and your whole body does a full-system cringe.

Let me start with this: I hate therapy. Or at least, I hated what I thought therapy was. The awkward Zoom calls. The flat affect. The "mm hms" that felt less like empathy and more like someone pretending to be a therapist on a bad TV show.

If that's your current mental picture of therapy, I get why you're avoiding it. I did too. For years. What this chapter is really about is not "go to therapy, it fixes everything," but how to decide if you want it in your toolkit at all, how to suffer through the parts that actually help, and how it connects to the next piece of this field guide, which is learning to notice your own patterns on purpose instead of by accident.

This is a story for you if:

- You tried therapy once, hated it, and decided, "Yeah, that's not for me."
- You keep getting told you "should" go, but the idea makes you want to climb out of your skin, or a window
- You think therapy is for people who are "really messed up," not for you, who is just "kind of a disaster, but managing."

Let me spoil the ending.

You didn't fail therapy. Therapy failed you.

And also, therapy is still work. Not magic. Not vibes. Work.

The session that made me quit (again)

The last time I quit therapy, it was after one virtual session.

The call started, and from the first second, my whole body went, "Absolutely not." She had no personality, at least none that I could feel through the screen. She asked a lot of questions, responded with a lot of "mm hm," and somehow managed to feel both clinical and checked out at the same time.

I didn't feel like she cared. I didn't feel like I was a person to her. Mostly, I felt like I was paying to be interviewed by a robot that had read about feelings in a textbook, or, if you're a teen, like being sent to the school counselor who barely looks up from their notes. I lasted the hour. I closed my laptop. Then I quit.

In my head, the story went like this: "I tried. Therapy just doesn't work for me. Maybe I'm not 'therapizable.' Maybe I'm too much of a mess. Or maybe it's all just kind of useless."

That story felt true. It also kept me stuck.

What I thought therapy was for

Back then, I was going to therapy for a pretty simple reason: I wanted my pain to stop.

Not "understand it." Not "build capacity," as in have more energy and tools to handle hard stuff. Not "heal generational trauma," as in work on the painful patterns that keep getting passed down in my family, or whatever the internet is saying this week.

I wanted:

- Less anxiety
- Less sadness
- Fewer meltdowns
- Fewer fights
- Less… everything

In my head, therapy was customer service for feelings. I bring my broken brain to the desk, the professional presses some buttons, and I leave with a calmer, less annoying personality.

So every time I tried therapy and didn't instantly feel better, I logged that as failure. My failure. The therapist's failure. The whole system's failure.

What I hadn't yet understood was this very annoying fact: therapy is not supposed to make you feel better right away. At first, it often makes you feel worse.

That's not a sign it's not working. That's often a sign that it is.

Which is very rude, honestly.

You Are Not A Bad "Client"

If you have Baader-Meinhof level guilt about "failing" at therapy, let me offer you a reframe.

There are lots of ways therapy can "fail you" before it ever has a real chance to help:

- Wrong therapist. Someone who is technically fine, but not for you. You don't feel safe. You don't feel seen. You cannot get yourself to actually say the real stuff. That's not you being difficult. That is your nervous system doing a very effective risk assessment.
- Wrong format. Maybe virtual feels fake to you. Maybe in-person feels too intense. Maybe weekly is too often at first. Maybe it's not enough. If the container doesn't work for your life, you will unconsciously drag your feet.
- Wrong goal. If you secretly want therapy to turn you into a calm, shiny "normal" person, you will constantly feel like you're failing every time you feel big emotions. That's not a growth plan. That is a self-erasure plan with a co-pay.

None of that makes you a bad client.

It makes you a human person trying to do hard emotional work in a setup that is not actually built for you yet.

The part that actually is work

Here is the moment therapy stopped being this abstract thing I was ‘supposed’ to do and started being something I was actively in. I was sitting on my bi-weekly Zoom call, already halfway into what sounded to me like a childish-sounding rant about how much I hated therapy, how much I hated sounding so defeated in front of her, how raw and useless it made me feel. She listened, nodded, chuckled, and then just said, "That’s the fucking point, man," like she was telling me the weather. I stared at her, because excuse me, what?

Here is the annoying grown-up part. Therapy will not wander into your life, set up perfectly, and start healing you while you sit very still and cooperative.

You have to do at least three pieces of work that no therapist can do for you:

1. Admitting what you really want

Not the polite version. Not “I just want to communicate better” or “I want to be happier.” Those are fine, but they are often cover stories.

Maybe what you actually want is, “I want to stop feeling like I'm broken.” Or, “I want to not hate myself every time I rest.” Or, “I want to not explode at my partner and then spiral for three days.”

When you can say the real want out loud, therapy suddenly has something to aim at.

Until then, both you and your therapist are shooting in the dark and asking, “Is this helping?” with no shared definition of what “helping” actually means.

2. Accepting that it will feel bad first

This part is where most of us bail.

You finally get a therapist you don't hate. You start poking at something real. You leave the session feeling raw, or shaky, or weirdly angry at them for "making" you think about hard things.

And a part of your brain goes, "See? This is making everything worse. Abort mission."

What's actually happening is closer to this: Your mind has spent years building elaborate systems to not feel certain things. To not think about specific memories. To not notice certain patterns.

Therapy starts turning on the lights in rooms you locked years ago. Of course it feels worse. You're seeing more.

That spike in discomfort is not failure. It's data. It says, "You are finally touching the thing you came here for."

3. Choosing your therapist on purpose

You are allowed to be picky. You are allowed to treat therapists like you would any other long-term collaborator.

If you don't feel safe with someone, that's not you "self-sabotaging." That's useful information.

The work here is:

- Noticing how your body reacts to them
- Listening when something in you goes, "Nope."
- Giving yourself permission to try someone else

You are not auditioning for them. You're interviewing them for a very important job. The job is "help my brain not eat me alive all the time."

So, did therapy actually help?

Here is the twist I didn't expect.

When therapy finally did start helping, it wasn't because I found the Magical Perfect Therapist who "got" me right away.

It was because:

- I stopped expecting them to fix me
- I started being honest about what I wanted out of it
- I let myself hate parts of the process and still show up

I still sometimes leave sessions annoyed. I still sometimes get angry. I still sometimes want to quit. I still sometimes tell my therapist that I hate her and our sessions. (Sorry, by the way!)

But the overall direction of my life has shifted. I understand myself better. I explode less. I come back from spirals faster. I can say "this hurts" without also saying "and it means I'm a failure as a person."

That didn't happen in one breakthrough moment. It happened in dozens of sometimes boring, occasionally very painful conversations where I kept showing up long enough for the work to do something.

If you're therapy-curious and terrified

If you are hovering at the edge of therapy, here's what I want you to know:

- Feeling scared to start is normal. Your brain isn't broken for reacting that way.
- Quitting after a bad fit isn't a sign you "can't do therapy." It's a sign you might need a different therapist, a different goal, or a different pace.
- Therapy is not a reward for being "sick enough." It's a tool for being less alone inside your own head.

Most of all, I want you to understand and feel this one thing, in your core: You did not fail therapy.

You just haven't had a version of therapy that is truly built for you, yet. You're allowed to go back. You're allowed to ask for more. You're allowed to treat yourself as someone worth the work.

Whichever route you take, the next chapter will help you make awareness less exhausting and more useful.

Therapist Kept Saying "Awareness." I Thought It Was Bullshit.

You know that moment in therapy when your therapist says, "Let us slow down and build some awareness around this" and your brain instantly goes, "Cool, so nothing useful today then?"

You're not alone in that.

For my first few months of therapy, I heard the word awareness and translated it as homework with no real reward. It sounded vague and kind of useless. I wanted tools, strategies, hacks. I wanted the therapist version of a YouTube tutorial, not a guided tour of my own feelings.

So if you've been nodding along in sessions while secretly thinking, "Awareness sounds like bullshit", this is for you.

In this chapter, we're not fixing your entire life. We're just going to get very clear on what "awareness" actually means and what is worth noticing in the first place. Think of it as learning how to read your own dashboard lights, so later, when we talk about wiring and habits and settings, you actually know what is blinking.

Then, in the later chapters, we will use that awareness to talk about how your brain is wired, which parts are solid hardware and which parts you can tweak, and how to turn all of that into actual adjustments instead of just vibes.

Awareness is not about fixing your brain

Here's where a lot of us get tangled. When I say "awareness," I don't mean:

- Learning enough about yourself so you can finally act like a neurotypical person
- Collecting evidence about how you're "too much" or "not enough."
- Proving that your struggles are your fault because "you should have known better."

To be direct, that is shame, dressed in self-improvement clothing.

When therapists talk about awareness, what they usually mean is something closer to this: Noticing what is actually happening inside you, in real time, so you can respect your brain rather than fight it.

Awareness is not "how do I fix myself". Awareness is "how does this system, meaning your brain and body together, actually run". It's like realizing your phone battery isn't trash, you're just running fifteen heavy apps at once with the brightness on max, and oh, you forgot to plug it in last night because ADHD got the best of you. Awareness is you finally opening the settings and going, "Oh. This is why it keeps dying at 3 p.m."

You are not the problem. The lack of a manual is the problem.

Awareness of what is impacting you

One big piece of this user guide is awareness of what is actually hitting you.

A lot of neurodivergent people move through the day like this: everything feels "a lot," then suddenly there's a meltdown or a shutdown or a quiet disappearing act. A meltdown, meaning an intense emotional outburst where you might cry, yell, or feel out of control. A shutdown, meaning you go quiet, numb, or freeze and cannot respond, even if you want to. From the outside, it looks like it came out of nowhere. From the inside, it can initially feel like that too.

Except it didn't come from nowhere. There were ten, twenty, thirty small impacts you didn't clock. Tiny drains on the battery. Things like:

- The background hum of a light that your friend doesn't even hear
- Having to make three last-minute changes to plans
- Being "on" socially for an extra hour
- A smell that makes your whole body tense, even if you keep smiling

If you're not aware of those impacts, your brain just files the whole thing under "I am weak" or "I overreacted."

Awareness lets you tell a different story. More like, "I walked through a sensory obstacle course while juggling social expectations and five task switches. Of course my system crashed."

Same events. Completely different meaning.

And meaning matters, because that is what decides whether you go into shame or into planning.

Awareness of how you feel

This is the classic therapist moment.

They ask, “And how did you feel when that happened?” You stare at the table and think, "I don't know, tired maybe? Fine? Annoyed? Hungry? All of the above?" You offer a word that sounds correct, and they gently stare at you like there is more.

And there usually is. And honestly, how fucking dare they somehow know me better than myself?

Neurodivergent people often get very good at tracking other people and very bad at tracking themselves. You may be tuned into:

- What the other person needs
- The vibe in the room
- The “right” reaction you're supposed to have

Meanwhile, your actual feelings are sitting in a corner holding a “notice me” sign. Awareness of how you feel is not some fluffy bonus skill. It is data. It is your live dashboard. “Fine” is not data. “Anxious and bracing for something to go wrong” is data. “Angry because my boundary just got run over” is data. “Overstimulated and starting to float away from my body” is data.

When you can name what you feel with a bit more precision, you get access to different options. You stop jumping straight to “push through” or “blow up” or “shut down”. You start to notice there are moves in between, like pausing, asking for help, changing the plan, or stepping away on purpose.

Awareness of where you need help

This is the part that usually stings.

Because many of us were trained, directly or indirectly, to believe that needing help is a failure, so we become experts at not noticing where we are drowning.

If you don't notice you need help, then you never have to risk asking. You never have to risk hearing no.

You also never get support.

Awareness is what lets you say things like:

- "Transitions are really hard for me. I need more time than you do."
- "I lose track of tasks once they leave my visual field. I need things written down or in a shared app."
- "If you call me without warning, I probably won't answer. I need a heads-up text."

This is not about making a list of your flaws. This is about mapping the hard parts of the terrain so you can build actual paths through it. And here is something important. Awareness is not just for your inner life. It is also how you give neurotypical people a bridge to you.

You can tell someone, "I'm struggling." They might care a lot and still not know what to do. If instead you can say, "Here is what is hard for me, and here is what helps," you are suddenly speaking a language they can act on. Awareness turns vague suffering into clear requests: "Crowds scramble my brain. Can we go at a quieter time?" "I am at the end of my sensory rope. I love you, I just need a low-input night." "I want to have this talk, I just need ten minutes to regulate first."

Awareness gives you that vocabulary. And vocabulary gives you options.

Three tiny prompts to build awareness

Okay, cool, awareness is magical and life-changing and all that. But how do you actually grow it without feeling like you are doing a full therapy session every time you stand in a line?

Start small. Stupid small. We're not writing a memoir; we're just adding a few more lines to the user manual.

Here are three simple prompts you can use in real time:

1. "What just changed for me?" You're doing mostly okay, then suddenly you're not. Ask this. Did a sound start? Did someone come into the room? Did the topic of conversation shift? Did you remember something stressful? You are training your brain to notice cause-and-effect in your own system.

2. "Where in my body am I clenching?" Do a quick scan. Jaw, shoulders, stomach, hands. You don't have to relax it, just notice. This moves awareness away from pure thoughts and into your actual nervous system, where many of your early warning signals live.

3. "What would make this 10 percent easier?" Not perfect. Not fixed. Just 10 percent easier. Maybe that's stepping outside for two minutes, putting in one earbud, lowering the brightness, or asking one small thing from someone. This shifts you from judging yourself to supporting yourself.

You can run through these prompts while you're in line at the store, sitting at your desk, or messaging someone back. They're awareness, but bite-sized.

Be curious about one thing that bugged you today

Let's keep this as real as possible.

When you close this book, I don't want you to remember every sentence. I would love it, though, if you did one small experiment.

Today, take one thing that bugged you. It can be tiny.

You snapped at a text. You bailed on a plan. You got stuck scrolling for an hour and felt gross after. You felt oddly drained after a chat with someone.

Instead of going straight to, "What is wrong with me?" try this:

- What was actually impacting me there?
- How was I feeling before, during, and after?
- Where did I maybe need help and didn't get it?

You're not looking for a perfect answer. You're just practicing curiosity instead of judgment.

That is awareness work.

You're teaching your brain that your reactions are not random failures. They're responses from a system that is doing its best with the information and support it has.

Awareness makes you kinder and clearer

The real payoff of all of this is not that you become some hyper-conscious monk who narrates every emotion in real time. Nobody has the bandwidth for that, and also, no thank you.

The payoff is that awareness slowly shifts two huge things.

You become kinder to yourself. Less, "Why am I like this?" and more, "Wow, no wonder that was hard." Shame turns into planning. Self-hatred turns into problem-solving. You start to respect your brain instead of bullying it.

And you become clearer with other people, especially the neurotypical ones. Instead of expecting them to magically understand your internal chaos, you can say: "Here is what is hard for me." "Here is what helps."

That clarity makes it easier for the right people to show up for you, and easier to spot when someone doesn't actually care to try.

You are still you. Same brain. Same wiring. The difference is that you are no longer flying blind inside your own life.

Your awareness is the manual you were missing

If you have spent years hearing "awareness" and quietly thinking, "That sounds fake and useless," I get it.

But awareness is not a soft skill that therapists made up to pass the time.

Your awareness is the user manual you were missing.

Not to turn you into somebody else, but to help you finally understand you. So you can stop apologizing for existing, start planning for how your brain actually works, and ask for the help you genuinely need.

Your awareness is not bullshit. It is how you learn to treat yourself like someone worth taking care of.

Now that you can spot what is happening, the next question is what can actually change. The next chapter looks at how your brain learns and what is realistically malleable.

You Can Change Your Brain (But Not Your Wiring)

Picture this.

You. Couch. Beer in hand. Doom scrolling reels, trying to forget what happened today, while your brain runs ten background tabs about tomorrow's work schedule and whether you said something weird three Tuesdays ago.

You're exhausted, but your brain is not getting the memo. You stumble across a video about neuroplasticity. The brain can rewire itself, they say. New habits. New pathways. New you. Maybe, you think, if you just do this right, you can finally stop being like this.

This guide is the gentle, slightly sarcastic voice that appears right then and says: Your brain is not broken. It is also not a blank slate you can rewrite from scratch.

Both are true.

What "rewiring your brain" actually means

If you've been trying to 'rewire' yourself into normal, this is the part that will save you from burning out again. Let's start with the shiny word: neuroplasticity.

People online talk about it like it's Hogwarts for your neurons. Learn the right spell, and suddenly you are a brand new person who loves spreadsheets and never forgets to reply to emails.

What it actually means is much simpler and, in a quiet way, more powerful.

Your brain is made of cells called neurons that talk to each other through little connections. When you do something over and over, those connections get stronger. When you stop doing something, some of those connections get weaker. That is neuroplasticity. Your brain is always adapting, learning patterns, shaping itself around what you repeatedly experience.

A super very important note, though: adapting is not the same as transforming into a different brain type.

Neuroplasticity is really good at:

- Building skills
- Forming habits
- Changing how you cope, respond, and pay attention

It is not the "off" switch for autism or ADHD. It does not uninstall your operating system. It just lets you install better apps, remove some malware, and clean up the desktop a bit.

Your brain is wired differently, not incorrectly

If you're autistic, ADHD, AuDHD, or otherwise interestingly wired, there is a specific setup in how your brain works. How you notice details. How you process sound, light, and social vibes. How you move between tasks. How your nervous system handles stress. Earlier, we talked about this as a different design, not a bad copy of a "normal" brain.

This chapter is about what that actually means for change. Which parts are hardwired enough that trying to "fix" them just burns you out, and which parts are flexible, trainable, or open to new habits. In other words, how neuroplasticity, practice, and environment can shift how you live with this wiring, without turning you into a different person.

You probably know this on some level. You have lived with:

- Needing extra stimulation just to focus
- Needing quiet like a calm little pond while the world blasts bad elevator music at full volume
- Going from zero to meltdown when a tiny thing tips you over, and not being able to "just get over it" no matter how hard you try

These are not signs that your brain is broken. They are signs that your baseline settings are not the same as the people who write most self-help books.

Neuroplasticity will not turn an autistic brain into a non-autistic brain. It will not "fix" ADHD by turning you into someone who loves filling out forms and thrives in open-plan offices. That is not failure. That is just reality.

The good news is that different wiring can still learn, grow, and make living in it easier. You don't need a new brain. You need new agreements with the one you have.

Habits, substances, and the stories they tell your brain

Back to you on the couch, beer in hand.

There is this quiet fear a lot of us have. If I drink, smoke, or scroll too much, am I "rewiring" my brain in some permanent, horrible way? Or the flip side: if I meditate, sleep eight hours, and cold plunge, will that finally make me "normal"?

Here is the less dramatic, more honest version.

Everything you do sends signals to your brain about what to expect.

When you drink every night to shut off the noise, your brain learns, "Ah, this is how we cope." It builds a path which looks like: Stress → Drink → Numb. That path can get pretty solid over time. It's not a moral failure to have that path. It's just how brains work. The brain notices what takes the edge off and tries to automate it.

When you quit, or cut down, your brain does not instantly delete the path. It slowly weakens while you build new ones, such as: Stress → Text a friend, Stress → Go outside, or Stress → Cry on the couch without adding alcohol to the mix. None of those look as shiny in a reel, but they are real plasticity. You are teaching your brain; we have other options now.

Same with scrolling. Your brain learns that little bursts of novelty equal "feel slightly less awful." So it goes back. And again. And again. You are not broken for doing this. You're a human with a nervous system trying to self-regulate using the tools that were easiest to reach.

This is also why the basics, like sleep, food, and movement, matter so much. Not because they magically cure your neurotype, but because they change how flexible your brain can be. A sleep-deprived, hungover, underfed brain can still change, it's just trying to do it while wearing ankle weights and noise-cancelling headphones that play static.

You are not turning yourself into a different person with every habit. You are deciding which paths in your existing forest get the most traffic.

What can actually change

So if your wiring is not going to flip to "normal," what is on the table?

Well... it turns out, a lot. You can change how your traits show up in daily life. You can:

- Learn what overstimulates you and design your life to avoid it when possible
- Build routines that support your brain instead of punishing it
- Practice noticing early warning signs before you hit shutdown or meltdown territory
- Create better scripts and skills for social stuff, if you want or need to

All of that is neuroplasticity. Your brain learns patterns like:

- "I am starting to buzz. I know if I keep going, I will crash. Time to take a break now, not in three hours."
- "I have one brain for planning and another for doing. Let me work with that instead of yelling at myself for procrastinating."
- "I do not have infinite spoons for noise, people, and decisions. I am allowed to say no earlier."

Over time, those new responses become easier. Not perfect, not automatic in every situation, but easier. That's not you faking being someone else. That's you becoming someone whose starting to learn their own system a little bit better.

The traits are still there. You still think in 27 parallel threads, or lose track of time, or hyperfocus so hard you forget to drink water.

The difference is that you and your brain are communicating instead of fighting.

Working with your not-broken brain

Here is the core shift.

The goal is not "how do I become normal." The goal is "how do I build a life that fits this brain?" Instead of "rewire it into something else," try "collaborate with what is already here." That can look like:

- Accepting that you will always need more recovery time than people who are not constantly running social and sensory analysis in the background, and planning your week around that

- Owning that your focus works in bursts, not steady streams, and structuring tasks in sprints instead of long marathons of suffering

- Realizing that your sensitivity is not just a weakness. It is also why you notice patterns, see risks early, care deeply, and pick up vibes other people miss

This is not toxic positivity. Some of this wiring is a genuine pain. Sometimes you will wish you could mute your brain, switch bodies, opt out of humaning for a bit. That is allowed. You don't have to love every part of it to stop calling it broken.

You can still change. You are changing, all the time, with every habit, every choice, every random Tuesday night on the couch when you put the beer down five minutes earlier and decide to actually feel your feelings instead of outrun them.

That is neuroplasticity, too. Tiny, unglamorous, real.

The message I want your brain to keep

If your brain remembers nothing else from this book, let it be this: You are not a failed version of someone else's brain.

You are a complete, specific, not-broken human with a nervous system that has its own rules.

Neuroplasticity will not turn you into a different species. It will not erase your autism or ADHD or whatever mix of letters you're made of. It will help you build new ways to cope, connect, rest, and work that do not hurt you as much.

You are already living in a brain that changes. The question isn't "can I rewire myself into normal," it is "what do I want my brain to get really good at from here?"

Self-hate is one pattern. Self-understanding is another. You get to choose which one you keep practicing.

From here, we'll move into what peace can look like for a brain like yours, not by forcing it to be quiet, but by giving it better ways to rest.

Why Your Brain Never Goes Quiet (And What Peace Can Actually Look Like)

Building on how brains change, here is what peace looks like when your mind never goes quiet. You know that moment when someone says, very casually, "I just sort of…stop thinking for a while" and your whole nervous system goes, "umm, I'm sorry, you what??

The way some people describe their mind going blank on purpose, like a calm TV that is simply turned off, can feel surreal. If your brain lives at a constant hum, that can sound less like "relaxation" and more like science fiction. If your inner world looks more like:

- random sounds
- replaying events from three days ago
- and pre-planning next Tuesday

then this is for you.

You are not broken. Your brain is just doing something very specific.

It's just not doing "quiet."

The fantasy of the blank mind

A lot of self-help content quietly assumes a certain kind of brain. There is this unspoken idea that a "healthy" mind will sometimes be empty. No thoughts. Just stillness.

For some people, that really is a thing. Their internal volume actually turns down. They can sit on the couch and genuinely think of nothing for a minute. Or five. Or twenty.

If that's not how your mind works, you can spend years trying to chase this mythical blank space. You lie in bed, listening to your thoughts whirl, and think, "Why will you not shut up?" You try the breathing exercises. You try "clear your mind." Your mind responds by producing a fresh playlist of intrusive jingles, detailed travel plans, and a full re-run of That One Conversation From 2019.

You are not failing. You are just using the wrong fantasy.

What "never quiet" actually looks like

Let us name some of what might be happening in there.

You might get random sounds, like your brain is cycling through audio files in no particular order. Snippets of a song. A line from a show. A noise you heard earlier. A word, repeated because the syllables feel interesting.

At the same time, another part of you is replaying events. You rewatch a conversation and notice tiny details. The tone. The timing. The exact moment you think you sounded odd. Your brain pauses, rewinds, edits the scene, then plays the "better" version. Again.

None of this means you are doing awareness wrong. It just means your brain does not do "blank screen," it does "27 tabs open with the volume up." So instead of chasing an empty mind you are never going to get, we are going to talk about what peace can actually look like for you. Fewer tabs. Lower volume. One thing at a time for a few seconds longer than you are used to.

Layered under that is the pre-planning. Working out how you will get to next week's appointment. Mentally walking through the route. Checking for possible problems. Who will be there? What will you wear? How tired will you be after? What will you eat beforehand so you don't crash in the middle?

You are basically running:

- a media player
- a court transcript
- and a logistics app

all at once.

To someone who has long, quiet gaps in their day, this sounds extreme. To many neurodivergent people, this sounds like Tuesday before lunch.

Why your brain keeps doing this

Here is the important part. Your brain is not talking just to annoy you. It is trying to take care of you.

For many neurodivergent folks, the world comes in louder and sharper. Sounds, light, textures, expressions, rules, and other people's moods. There is a lot of data. Your brain learns early that it has to process constantly just to keep up.

So it builds habits.

- The "random sounds" can be a kind of internal stimming. Background noise that helps you regulate when the outside noise feels unpredictable.

- The replaying of events is often a safety check. Your system goes back over what happened to scan for danger, shame, or a missed rule, because in the past, that might have kept you safe.
- The future planning is a full risk assessment tool. It tries to predict every possible problem so you don't get caught off guard.

This is protective. It is also exhausting.

If you grew up needing to track social rules, hidden expectations, or shifting emotions around you, your brain got very good at staying on. It did it to keep you out of trouble. To avoid humiliation. To reduce sensory overload. To plan an exit.

So now, when someone says, "Just relax, let your mind go blank," your brain hears, "Stop scanning for danger," and it politely declines.

Your brain is loyal. It's doing what it was trained to do.

What if peace is not the same as silence

The problem is not that your brain is active. The problem is that the way we talk about "peace" is too narrow. If we define peace as "no thoughts at all," then anyone whose brain is wired for constant background processing will always feel like a failure. That is not fair and not accurate.

Think about quiet in a different way.

There is the silence of an empty field. No movement. No sound. Then there is the quiet of a room where someone is typing softly. A kettle in the next room. A clock ticking. There are sounds, but they're steady. Predictable. They don't spike your nervous system.

Your mind might never be an empty field, though it can still become more like that second room.

Peace, for you, might look like:

- Your thoughts staying in one lane long enough that you can follow them
- The background noise shifting from "panic planning" to "gentle hum"
- Being able to notice, "Oh, my mind has picked up that old memory again," without getting dragged all the way into it

That counts. That is real peace.

Small ways to work with a busy brain

Standard advice often says, "Push the thoughts away. Empty your mind." If that has never worked for you, you are in good company.

Instead of trying to make your brain turn off, you can experiment with giving it better jobs. One simple shift is to move from "stop thinking" to "single-task thinking." Your brain wants to run. Fine. Give it one path. You can try things like:

- Focusing on one repeating phrase or sound on purpose, and letting everything else become background noise. You're not chasing the other thoughts away; you just keep returning to the one you picked.
- Writing your pre-planning down in a list, even a messy one. This tells your system, "The plan is saved. You don't have to hold all of it at once."
- Setting a gentle boundary with your replay brain. For example, telling yourself, "I will think about that conversation for the next five minutes," and then shifting

to a sensory task, like feeling your feet on the floor or the weight of a blanket.

None of this creates a blank void. It just reduces mental traffic jams.

Your brain still gets to be itself. It just has a little more structure.

Redefining goals: from "off switch" to "dimmer switch"

If you go into this with the goal of "I want a totally empty mind," you will probably keep feeling stuck. For many neurodivergent brains, that is not a realistic or even a safe feeling target.

A more honest goal might be, "I want my brain to have a dimmer switch."

You may not turn the lights off, but you can lower the brightness. That could mean:

- Taking the edge off the constant planning so you can fall asleep faster
- Turning down the emotional volume on old memories, even if they still pop up
- Letting random sounds exist in the background without also running a full drama analysis at the same time

None of this requires you to become a different kind of person. It just asks your protective system to use less fuel when it can.

When you stop demanding silence, your nervous system can actually start to relax. It no longer has to fight you while it tries to protect you.

You are not a broken radio

If your brain never goes quiet, you might secretly fear that you are damaged. Like everyone else got a mind that has an "off" button, and you got stuck with a radio that plays twenty stations at once.

What you actually have is a highly tuned, always-on system that learned to keep you safe by staying alert. That constant stream of sounds, replays, and plans is not proof that you are failing at being calm. It is proof that you adapted.

You can absolutely teach that system new rhythms. Not by shaming it into silence but by respecting why it works the way it does, then slowly showing it that some moments are safe enough to be softer.

Peace, for you, does not have to look like a blank white room.

It can look like a busy but friendly station, where the announcements are clear, the schedule is written down, and even if there is always something happening, you can breathe in the middle of it.

Your brain may never go completely quiet. It can still be your ally. And it can still learn what your version of peace feels like.

When One Beer Makes the World Quiet

There is a moment after work where my whole nervous system feels like a buzzing power line.

Emails still echo in my head. Tiny mistakes replay. My body feels half-braced, like it's waiting for something bad to happen. Lights are too bright. People are too loud. Even my own thoughts feel like a room full of conversations happening at once.

So I leave.

I go out, order one beer, maybe two. I sit alone. I scroll my phone. I just exist for a bit. No forced small talk. No pretending. No performing calm. Just me, the chair, the glass, and a low hum of background noise that, for once, does not feel like an attack.

Then the first sip hits.

My shoulders drop. My thoughts line up, just a little. The world feels softer around the edges. And for the first time all day, my brain goes quiet enough that I can hear myself think.

If one drink feels like the only time your brain shuts up, this chapter is not here to shame you. It is here to explain why that relief feels so real, why it is so tempting, and why it can quietly turn into something that feels complicated fast.

Not to romanticize it. Not to lecture you. Just to understand it.

You are not broken for liking the quiet

First, a small act of mercy.

You are not a bad person for liking how alcohol makes you feel.

If your baseline state is overstimulated, anxious, or permanently on guard, it makes complete sense that something which slows your system down feels like relief. The world tends to treat that as a moral flaw. Your nervous system treats it as, finally, a break.

If you grew up being told you were too much or too sensitive, you probably learned early that your raw self was not safe. You learned to control your reactions, tone things down, and keep your internal chaos hidden so you would be easier for others to handle.

That is not a personality quirk. That is a full-time security job inside your own skull.

So by the time the workday ends, or the kids are asleep, or the laptop finally closes, you are not just tired. You are hijacked. Your brain has been scanning for threat, judgment, and rejection all day, filing everything away for replay at 3 a.m.

Then you take a sip.

And your whole system goes, "Oh. This."

What alcohol is actually doing to your brain

Let's keep the science simple.

Alcohol is a central nervous system depressant. That means it slows things down. Not just reaction time or coordination, but the nonstop firing inside your head. It increases GABA, a chemical that quiets overactive signals.

If you're neurodivergent, your baseline might already look like this:

- Sensory input turned up too high
- Emotional volume stuck near max
- Thoughts running 30 tabs at once with no mute button

So what feels "normal" to you may already be far above what others experience.

Then you drink.

Signals that were screaming turn into a low murmur. The internal commentary loses its grip. Background noise stops feeling like an assault. Your body unclenches. Conversations feel possible instead of exhausting.

Alcohol does not always make you feel less. Sometimes, it makes you feel enough.

Enough to sit still. Enough to talk. Enough to stop replaying the email you sent without the attachment, even though Outlook tried to warn you.

That is the part people rarely say out loud.

Too much and not enough, at the same time

Here is the strange double bind many neurodivergent people live in.

Sometimes you drink because you feel too much. Too many thoughts. Too much shame. Too much sound. Too much tension buzzing under your skin.

Other times, you drink because you feel like you're not enough.

Not relaxed enough to be around people. Not confident enough to speak freely. Not “normal” enough to drop the armor.

The same drink can seem to solve both.

That mild buzz acts like a temporary settings menu for your brain. Anxiety down. Self-criticism down. Social fear down. The “I am a weird alien in a human costume” feeling down.

It doesn't turn you into someone else. It removes some of the blockers between you and the version of you that feels most real.

Of course that feels like a hug. Of course your brain wants to remember that hug.

Why the hug feels risky

Here is the hard part.

Alcohol is doing something for your nervous system that the world should have helped you do in other ways.

You should have had spaces where you didn't have to mask so hard. You should have had people who didn't demand calm, quiet, or constant professionalism. You should have been taught ways to regulate your nervous system that didn't require a bar tab.

Instead, many of us heard things like:

- “Why are you so dramatic?”
- “Just try harder to focus.”
- “You can’t make everything about your feelings.”

So you built your own workaround.

You learned that a drink lets you lower your guard. That you can tolerate the grocery store, the work event, or the family gathering without planning an escape route. And even if you aren't getting drunk, even if nothing on paper looks alarming, there is often a quiet unease underneath.

"If I need this to feel like myself, what does that say about me?"

Here is my answer, and you can try it on.

It says more about the conditions you are living in than about your character or willpower. Your brain found something that worked fast and reliably. It grabbed it because there weren't many other tools within reach.

That doesn't make alcohol harmless, though. But it does make your relationship with it understandable.

How the pattern forms

Your brain is always learning.

This is neuroplasticity in plain language. The more you repeat something, the easier that path becomes. Drink once in a while to calm down, and your brain notes it as an option. Drink after every hard day, and your brain upgrades it to the default.

It learns:

- When we feel like this, we drink
- When we can't slow down, we drink
- When sleep feels impossible, we drink

Neurodivergent brains are especially good at patterns. Strong routines. Strong associations. Deep grooves. So when alcohol joins the routine, it does not stay a casual side character. It becomes part of the main script.

That is not a moral failing. It is wiring.

The gray space no one talks about

There is a cultural picture of problem drinking that looks like chaos. Missed work. Broken relationships. Obvious damage.

So if your experience looks more like:

- "I have one or two drinks most nights and really look forward to them."
- "I feel more like myself with a drink than without."
- "When I try to cut back, life feels unbearably raw."

You can end up stuck in a gray space. Too functional to panic. Too dependent to ignore.

Especially if you're neurodivergent. Because for us, the choice is often not between fun and excess. It is between being constantly overwhelmed and being slightly dulled, in a way that finally feels manageable.

That is a different equation. You are not the only one doing that math every evening.

Curiosity instead of cruelty

If you recognize yourself here, I hope you walk away with a few things.

First, language: So when shame pops up with that first sip, you can say, "My nervous system is fried, and this is currently the fastest way I know to turn the volume down." That is not an excuse. It is context.

Second, permission to be curious instead of cruel: You do not have to label yourself. You also do not have to pretend nothing is happening. You are allowed to notice patterns without punishing yourself for them.

Third, self-compassion that actually fits: Not the fluffy kind. The grounded kind. The kind that says, “Of course you reached for the one thing that reliably gave you peace.”

You deserve regulation. You deserve softness. You deserve a nervous system that is not constantly screaming. If alcohol gives you a shadow version of that, it makes sense that it feels comforting.

You are not weak for wanting the hug.

You are a neurodivergent person living in a world that often sets your brain on fire, and you found one of the few fire extinguishers within reach.

You get to look at it clearly. You get to decide what kind of relationship you want with it. You get to want more for yourself than the bottom of a glass.

And you do not have to be ashamed that, for now, because for now, this is how you make it through the evening.

Try saying this, quietly, like a note to your own brain: Dear neurodivergent brain, you are doing the best you can with what you were given. You are allowed to want better.

That first sip feels like a private mercy. When the brain files it as a repeatable solution, patterns form. Hold on to that idea of the relief loop, because your brain can build the same “this is how we cope now” pathway with other things too.

NEUROSPICY STONERS: A FIELD GUIDE TO YOUR HIGH ND BRAIN

You know that moment at night when your body is tired, but your brain is like, "Cool, anyway, here is every mistake you have ever made plus ten new ideas for apps you'll never build"?

This is where a lot of neurodivergent folks meet weed.

Not at a party. Not in some wild story.

On the couch. In bed. Alone with a loud brain that just won't shut up.

Once you've seen how your brain and alcohol can get into a relief loop together, it can be hard to unsee that pattern. Overwhelm, then something that makes the world a little softer, then your brain quietly filing that away as, "Oh, this is how we cope now." The same story plays out with other substances, too, just with different buttons pressed and different side effects.

For some neurodivergent brains, alcohol takes the edge off social panic and "being on" in front of other people. Weed often aims more at the late-night mental noise, the racing thoughts, the internal monologue that never finds the off switch. That is the pattern we are going to pull apart in this chapter.

This chapter is about what is actually going on in that brain when you get high, especially if you are ADHD, autistic, AuDHD, or just generally in the "spicy brain" category.

Not to scare you. Not to tell you to stop. To help you understand what you are doing, so you can choose it on purpose instead of feeling like it is choosing you.

Why neurodivergent brains and weed keep finding each other

If you have a neurodivergent brain, you are already living life on "hard mode" in some way. You might be juggling:

- Runaway thoughts that refuse to slow down when it's time to sleep
- Background anxiety that hums even when nothing is technically wrong
- Sensory overload, where the world is just too loud, bright, or much
- Time blindness, so day and night blur together until it's suddenly 2 a.m.

Now drop weed into that mix. It often does three things very fast:

- Turns the volume down on your thoughts
- Softens the edges of your anxiety
- Makes your body feel heavier, safer, maybe even cozy

That can feel like magic. Or medicine. Or both. If your whole day has been white-knuckle self-control, masking, and fighting your brain, it makes sense that when you finally get to choose how you feel, you reach for the thing that works.

You weren't "weak" for doing that. You were responsive. You noticed what helped and you used it.

Weed 101: What it's doing in there

To understand why neurodivergent brains often have a big "ohhhh yes" reaction to weed, it helps to know a tiny bit about the system it talks to.

Your brain and body have something called the endocannabinoid system. It helps regulate things like:

- mood
- appetite
- pain
- memory
- sleep
- stress responses

Your body already makes its own cannabis-like chemicals to keep all this in balance. THC and CBD, the main active bits in weed, plug into parts of that same system.

When THC shows up, it can:

- shift how you feel time, so the moment you are in feels bigger
- quiet certain kinds of brain chatter
- boost some kinds of sensory pleasure
- scramble working memory a bit, so you are less locked into your usual thought loops

For many neurodivergent people, that last part is a feature, not a bug. Your default loops can be cruel. "Why did I say that?" "Why can't I do basic tasks?" "Why am I like this?" If weed can loosen that loop, even for an hour, of course, your brain remembers that it helped.

Neurodivergent brains: same plant, different playground

Here's where it gets interesting. The plant is the same. The brain it lands in is not. An ADHD or autistic brain often has differences in:

- dopamine signaling, which affects motivation, reward, and attention
- sensory processing, which affects what feels like "too much" or "too little"
- arousal regulation, which is the fancy way of saying "how revved up or shut down your body feels"

So when weed steps in and starts nudging those systems, the effects can hit differently than in a neurotypical brain.

If your baseline is "understimulated but overwhelmed," THC can feel like it finally syncs your brain and body. Your thoughts slow down just enough to catch them. Your senses soften just enough to feel safe.

Or, if your baseline is "nervous system on red alert," THC might let you relax for the first time all day. It can feel like someone took your internal alarm system and turned it from "siren" to "background hum."

The key idea here is this: You are not reacting to weed in a weird way. You are reacting with a different brain.

That matters because a lot of the advice out there about cannabis is built on how it shows up in neurotypical nervous systems. Your mileage is allowed to vary.

Weed and sleep: the off-switch you built yourself

Let us talk about the nighttime thing, because this is where many neurodivergent folks build their strongest weed habits. You try to sleep. Your brain says, "No thanks, what if we think instead?"

So you use weed as an off-switch.

From the outside, it might look like "you always need to be high to sleep." From the inside, it feels more like, "I finally found something that makes the torture at bedtime stop."

THC often helps people:

- fall asleep faster
- feel less stressed about the fact that they're not asleep yet
- shift attention from racing thoughts into body sensations, which feel safer

If you grew up being told you were "lazy" or "not trying hard enough," every missed night of sleep can feel like proof that something is wrong with you. Of course you are going to cling to anything that lets you skip that nightly shame spiral.

Here is the tricky part. Over time, your brain is very good at learning shortcuts. If you pair "weed" with "sleep" often enough, your brain can start to believe, "Weed is the only way we know how to sleep." The habit becomes part biology, part ritual, part fear of what happens if you don't use it.

This doesn't mean you must stop. It just means if you notice panic at the idea of sleeping without it, that is not you being dramatic.

That is your nervous system trying to protect you from going back to a state it remembers as painful.

Tolerance, dependence, and why that word feels gross

Quick note on terms, because they get thrown around and are often used to shame people.

- Tolerance just means your brain starts to adapt. Over time, you may need more weed to get the same effect. This is a normal brain process.
- Dependence means your body or brain gets used to something being around. If it's gone, you notice the difference in a way that can feel rough. Again, this is about adaptation, not moral failure.

If you have a neurodivergent brain, you already know what it's like to depend on outside things to function. Timers, meds, notes, white noise, the same YouTube video for the hundredth time. You build systems because your raw brain is not built for this world.

Weed can slide into that same category in your mind. "This is just my nighttime tool."

That frame is not wrong. It's just incomplete. A useful upgrade is: "This is one of my tools. It works in some ways, it costs in others. I get to decide if the trade is still worth it."

No shame. Just data.

Using weed like a scientist, not a villain or a saint

If the goal is informed choices, the main skill you want is curiosity. Not, "Is this bad?" More, "What is this doing for me, and what is it doing to me?"

Some questions you can quietly track for yourself over a week or two:

- What is my brain like right before I use it? (Anxious, bored, wired, lonely, overstimulated.)
- What changes in my body and thoughts 20–40 minutes after?
- How do I feel the next morning? Clearer, foggier, more motivated, less?
- Do I still enjoy sober time, or does everything feel "not quite right" unless I am a bit high?

You don't have to write a whole journal if that sounds like homework hell. Even mentally tagging patterns can help. "Ah, this kind of stress always makes me want to smoke." "This dose knocks me out, but I feel weird the next day."

The goal is not to catch yourself doing it "wrong." It's to become an expert in your own brain.

From there, small tweaks can make a big difference. Stuff like:

- Shifting timing, so you're not still super high at the exact moment you want deep sleep to kick in.
- Playing with lower doses if you only need your thoughts turned down, not completely deleted.
- Keeping at least some nights where you let yourself feel what sober sleep is like now, not what it was like years ago.

Again, this is not a secret command to change anything. It's more like saying, "Aim the thing on purpose."

Talking to doctors without wanting to scream

Neurodivergent people have a mixed history with doctors. You might have had:

- Your pain brushed off
- Your struggles blamed on "bad habits"
- Your self-knowledge dismissed because it didn't fit their idea of "normal"

So walking into a room and saying, "I use weed to sleep" can feel like offering them a loaded weapon they might aim at your character. You are allowed to protect yourself. You are also allowed to bring this up, because it is real, and it affects things like meds, sleep, and mood.

If you do talk to a doctor, a simple frame that can help is: "I am neurodivergent. I use cannabis most nights to help my brain wind down and sleep. It helps in these ways. I am also curious about how it might affect my sleep quality and my other meds. I am not looking for a lecture, just real information."

If you don't get a respectful, thoughtful response, that's not proof you were wrong to ask. It's just proof that this person doesn't get it yet. You deserve care that takes your actual brain, and your actual coping tools, into account.

You, weed, and the story you tell yourself

Under all the science, what really matters is the story in your head.

Is it:

"I am broken, so I need weed to function"?

or

“I have a different brain. Weed is one of the ways I manage that difference. I am allowed to use tools, and I am allowed to change them if and when I want”?

Those are very different stories.

The first one shrinks you. The second one keeps you in the center, with weed as a side character.

You are not a failure for needing help to sleep. You are not weak for wanting your brain to be kinder to you. You are not “bad at adulting” because you reach for a plant that makes life feel more livable.

You have a neurodivergent brain in a world that was not built for it. Of course you built yourself an off-switch. This chapter is just here to remind you: you are allowed to understand that switch, not just flip it in the dark.

Relaxants and stimulants both try to solve the same problem: an overworked nervous system. Next, we'll look at the socially accepted cousins of these coping tools, like caffeine and prescription meds, and why they behave oddly in our neurospicy systems.

Vyvanse, Coffee, and a Nap: My Neurodivergent Caffeine Story

You wake up already tired.

Not "ugh, it's Monday" tired. Ancient, soul-level, I just slept and yet tired kind of tired. So you do what you always do. You reach for the thing that's supposed to fix it. Coffee. Red Bull. Monster. Whatever your potion is. You drink it.

In the last few chapters, we talked about the obvious substances people use to manage their brains, like alcohol and weed, the ones that get moral panic headlines and awkward public health posters. Caffeine and meds live in the same general neighborhood; they are just the socially approved cousins with better branding and prescription labels.

You also take your Vyvanse, like the responsible, fully medicated creature you are.

And then, two hours later, your brain says, "Nap time." And you can actually fall asleep. Welcome to the weird little circus that is a neurodivergent nervous system on caffeine.

“How can I drink coffee and still nap?”

Let’s start with the part that makes neurotypical people look at us like we're glitching.

Neurodivergent Person: triple shot, ADHD meds, still sleepy enough to pass out. Neurotypical Person: “If I drink coffee after 3 p.m., I will see god at 2 a.m.”

The reason this feels so confusing is that most advice about caffeine is written for brains not running in hard mode.

A lot of us use caffeine like:

- A DIY focus potion so we can start anything at all
- A way to mask and be “on” in social or work settings
- A sensory regulator, because that sharp, buzzy hit cuts through brain fog and static

So on paper, caffeine is a stimulant, and stimulants are supposed to make you more awake. In a neurodivergent body, stimulants can do something weirder. They can help you finally relax enough to feel how tired you actually are.

You're not broken for this. You are not “so lazy that even coffee can’t fix you.” You're exhausted. And caffeinated. At the same time.

Both are true.

Your brain is not starting from neutral

Most caffeine advice quietly assumes you wake up at baseline. Like your body is a calm little pond, and coffee is the rock that makes the splash. Neurodivergent bodies usually don't wake up as calm little ponds. We wake up like:

- Heart already beating a bit fast
- Thoughts already doing laps
- Sensory system already scanning the room for "too bright, too loud, too much."
- A to-do list running in the background like bad elevator music

Caffeine then doesn't take you from zero to sixty. It takes you from "sixty but tired" to "seventy, focused, and still tired."

Sometimes that little bump helps your nervous system feel more organized. Thoughts line up. You can pick one thing. You stop bouncing from tab to tab. Your body reads that as safer, and when you feel safer, your brain finally lets you rest.

So yes, it can look like: Caffeine + meds → actually able to nap.

Not because caffeine is a sedative, but because for many neurodivergent folks, stimulation can be calming when your baseline is already chaos.

Caffeine as self-medication (that kind of works)

If you grew up with an undiagnosed neurodivergent brain, there is a very good chance you met caffeine way before you met any kind of formal support.

Of course you did. It's legal, cheap, praised in productivity culture, and available in a thousand cute flavors.

It also quietly does a lot of things that you feel like you need in a neurodivergent body:

- It can make a noisy, foggy brain snap into hyperfocus, at least for a bit.

- It can help you mask in social situations, because you can keep up with conversation and push through social exhaustion.
- It can buffer against sensory overwhelm. That crisp, caffeinated "edge" can cut through the cotton wool feeling when the world is too much.
- It gives you a predictable, reliable ritual. Same drink, same cup, same moment in your day. That's regulation too.

So when people say, "Wow, you drink a lot of coffee," your body hears, "Yes, because this is the closest thing I had to medicine for twenty years, Karen."

This isn't to scare you or to say caffeine is evil. This is to name that you were doing your best guess at self-support with what you had. And sometimes it helped. Enough that quitting or even cutting back could feel terrifying.

Because if this is what lets you function, who are you without it?

The hidden price tag: when your "little treat" eats your sleep

Here is where it gets sneaky.

You might be thinking, "If I can nap after caffeine, surely it's not ruining my sleep." Sleep is not just "can I pass out." It's also:

- How deeply you sleep
- How often you micro-wake without remembering
- Whether you hit the restful stages enough to feel alive in the morning

You can absolutely:

- Drink coffee
- Take your meds
- Nap
- And still have your overall sleep quality wrecked in the background

Which then makes you more tired. Which makes you reach for more caffeine.

Cue the loop where: You are exhausted, so you drink caffeine to function, which wrecks your sleep, which makes you more exhausted, which makes you drink more caffeine.

Your brain could read this as: “I am hopeless, lazy, and weak.” Your nervous system is quietly whispering: “I am tired and propped up on stimulants like a raccoon on a skateboard.”

Again, this is not you being dramatic. This is your body trying to keep up with the life settings you were handed.

“So do I have to quit coffee to be a real adult?”

Absolutely not.

You don't need to become a Green Juice Morning Person to be worthy. You also don't need to wait until you hit some imaginary rock bottom to experiment. Think of this less as “quitting caffeine” and more as “getting curious about how much it is actually helping you.”

A few gentle ideas you can borrow, ignore, or edit:

- Timing experiments. Keep your usual amount, but pull it earlier. Notice how your body feels if nothing caffeinated touches your face after, say, 1 or 2 p.m. You don't have to nail this every day for it to matter.

- Strength experiments. Same ritual, slightly less actual caffeine. Half-caff. Smaller size. One energy drink instead of two. Tiny, boring shifts. This is about sneaking under your own alarm system.
- Swap one, not all. If you drink three strong things a day, try swapping just one for something that still feels nice. A fun tea. A flavored sparkling water. Hot chocolate. Your brain still gets a treat and a ritual, just with a softer chemical impact.

The goal is not to be pure. The goal is to collect data on your own body.

If you try something for a week and feel exactly the same, great, you learned something. If you try something and notice you are even 10 percent less like a haunted baguette in the morning, that is useful too.

You are allowed to go slow. Glacial, even.

You are not broken for being tired

If caffeine "does nothing," yet you panic at the idea of losing it, that makes sense. You are not silly for leaning on the one thing that seemed to work in a world that was not built for your brain. You are also not doomed to live in a permanent state of wired and wiped, where your eyes are buzzing, but your soul is horizontal.

Your neurodivergent brain is not a boring, badly made brain. It is a sensitive, overclocked, creative little computer that has been running on survival settings for a long time.

Caffeine did not cause that. It just became part of the way you kept the system online.

If you ever decide you want to shift that relationship, you don't have to do it with shame or all-or-nothing rules.

You can do it like you do everything else: Chaotically. Experimentally. With ten tabs open. One tiny adjustment at a time.

And if all you get from this is the sentence, "I can be exhausted and caffeinated, and that doesn't make me a failure," that is already a pretty good place to start. Your energy drink doesn't have to give you wings; it just has to stop convincing you that needing help to function means you're broken.

Caffeine and meds are one side of the coping ledger. The other is the world itself: sudden sounds, bright lights, and aesthetics that make your nervous system snap. The next chapter steps out of substances and into those sensory trigger moments.

Why My Neurodivergent Brain Loses Its Shit At Loud Trucks

After spending a few chapters on the creative ways neurodivergent brains try to calm themselves down, I want to zoom out and look at something else. The flare-ups. The moments where your whole nervous system goes from "mostly fine" to "absolutely not" in half a second, often over something other people barely notice. This next bit gets loud and performative on purpose.

I keep telling myself I am a live-and-let-live person.

Wear what you want. Date who you want. Put glitter on your face. Shave half your head. Whatever.

And then a giant, lifted, screamingly loud truck rolls past, eating a lane and a half of road, and some feral part of my brain stands up on the table and starts yelling. Out loud if I'm alone or with someone close to me. Very much not out loud if I'm not.

It's like there's a tiny, profanity-powered sports commentator in my head, doing play-by-play on how unnecessary this vehicle is, how loud it is, how much space it takes up, what it might be compensating for, what it probably does to small animals and curbside mailboxes.

Loud trucks are just one example, but they're a clear case study of something many neurodivergent people live with every day. Sensory triggers that hit so hard and so fast they feel like moral offenses, not just “slightly annoying sounds.”

From the outside, I look calm. On the inside, it's an old-school Twitter thread. So what is going on there?

If you are neurodivergent and you have that same “I don’t care what people do, except suddenly I care A LOT” reaction to certain cars, sounds, or aesthetics, this is for you.

This is less about trucks, and more about that gap between your values and your reflex. Between who you think you are and how your nervous system responds in the moment.

Let us walk into that gap for a bit.

Two things can be true

First, the values part.

On purpose, you have decided: other adults get to make their own choices. If it's not hurting anyone directly, it's not your business.

You may even be proud of this. You worked hard to unlearn the judgment you were raised with or experienced around you in school growing up. You want to be accepting, especially because, as a neurodivergent person, you have been judged for things that were not really your choice.

Then there is the other part. The part that flares before you even know you saw the truck. The instant disgust. The tight jaw. The internal monologue that arrives fully written. That part is not a thoughtful moral stance. It is pattern recognition plus body response, happening at speed. Those two parts of you are not enemies. They just operate on different clocks.

Your values run at "slow conversation" speed. Your nervous system runs at "car backfires next to your ear" speed.

Of course the fast one gets there first.

Sensory input that feels like an attack

Let us talk about the sensory piece, because for a lot of neurodivergent folks, that is where the volume gets turned up.

A big, modified truck is not just a visual object. It is a sensory event. You get:

- The sound: low rumble, roar, or sharp, popping exhaust that slices through whatever you were thinking.
- The vibration: the way it shakes the ground or your chest as it idles or peels out.
- The visual chaos: extra height, strange proportions, aggressive angles, maybe bright lights.

If your sensory system is already working hard in daily life, that combo can feel like someone walked into your house, flipped on all the lights, and started clapping in your face.

From their side, they are "just driving." From your side, they have introduced a loud, unpredictable stimulus you did not consent to, right next to your body. Your brain does not file that under "oh hey, a fun lifestyle choice." It files it under threat. Not always danger in the "we are going to die" sense. More like danger in the "my system is now hijacked" sense.

You were maybe half-regulated, hanging in there, and suddenly this truck siphons off all your bandwidth just to process the noise, the vibration, the looming presence at the edge of your vision. Your reaction is not, "I disagree with lifted trucks as a concept." Your reaction is, "Make it stop."

By the time your values show up to say, "We are kind and chill and nonjudgmental," your nervous system is already lit up like a dashboard on fire.

Pattern recognition meets aesthetics

Even if the sound doesn't totally fry you, there is often an aesthetic pattern at work. Neurodivergent brains notice patterns. We live in them. We lean on them to predict what happens next so the world feels less chaotic. Over time, your brain has probably built a quiet little database that links "this type of vehicle" with "this type of behavior." Not because of one truck. Because of repetition.

Loud modified truck in your lane? Maybe there's tailgating. Or sudden braking. Or speeding past a crosswalk. Or rolling coal on cyclists. Or just general "I own this road" energy.

Your brain logs that. Over and over.

So when it sees the next big lifted truck, it's not just processing the image. It's also pulling up that whole cluster of past experiences at once. You are not looking at a truck. You are looking at: "Last week, when one of these screamed past the school zone." "And that time in the parking lot where one parked diagonally across two spaces." "And that day the engine revved next to you, and you flinched hard enough almost to spill your coffee."

Your nervous system goes, "Ah. I know this pattern. This is the 'unsafe, inconsiderate, loud, takes too much space' pattern."

So when you feel that intense "ugh" in your bones, it is not just about the current vehicle. It's the whole pattern history showing up at once.

Moral disgust gets in the mix

On top of the sensory overload and pattern recognition, there is another layer that often shows up for neurodivergent folks. Moral disgust.

You might care a lot about things like:

- Fairness
- Shared space
- Not wasting resources on pure show
- Not harming people around you just because you can

So when you see something that looks like a rolling monument to "my comfort and image matter more than everyone else's experience," your brain doesn't treat that as neutral. It feels like a violation of the social contract you are trying to live by. That is when the internal commentary gets spicy. Not just, "That is loud." More like, "Do you even see how much space you are taking? How much noise you are injecting into everyone's day? How much fuel you are burning to look like a tank at the grocery store?"

You are not mad at a machine. You are reacting to what the machine signals.

Even if that's not what the driver consciously means, your brain has linked this whole visual and auditory package to a set of values that clash with yours.

So now you have a triple stack:

- Sensory system yelling, "Too much, too loud, make it stop."
- Pattern system yelling, "We have seen this before, it went badly."

- Moral system yelling, “This feels unfair and selfish.”

No wonder the inner monologue is not rested and reasonable.

Values, impulses, and the “good person” trap

Here is where it gets uncomfortable.

Because many of us have a quiet rule running in the background: “If I were really a good, open-minded person, I would not have these ugly thoughts.” So now, on top of the original reaction, you stack shame about the reaction.

“I say I don't judge people, but listen to my brain right now.” “Why am I so mean about this? What is wrong with me?”

If that is you, I want to offer a reframe. There is a difference between what your nervous system spits out in the first half-second and what you choose to do with it.

You cannot values-train your way out of having a startle response to a truck that sounds like a dragon choking on fireworks. You also cannot logic your way out of the patterns your brain has built over years of experience. What you can do is notice that gap and decide how much authority each layer gets. You can say, “Wow, my whole body hates this,” without turning it into, “Therefore, that person is less human, and I am better.”

You can let yourself have the internal scream, then bring your values online for what happens next. No spiritual points are deducted for having a nervous system.

Making sense of your own reactions

So what do you actually do with this? Not in the “make yourself saintly” way. In the “live inside your own head with less confusion” way.

A couple of gentle places to experiment:

1. Name the layers. When a loud, visible, whatever-it-is rolls by and your brain flares, try mentally tagging the pieces.

“This is my sensory system panicking.” “This is my pattern brain making predictions.” “This is my moral brain getting loud about fairness.”

You don't have to fix them. Just sorting them can lower the internal drama.

2. Separate reaction from stance. You can react with disgust and still decide your actual stance is, “People get to have terrible taste and loud hobbies, but I want noise laws enforced.”

You don't have to collapse “my body hates this” into “that person is garbage” or “I am a monster for feeling this way.”

Both are shortcuts. Neither is accurate.

3. Notice when it is about capacity. If you are already overloaded, the same truck will hit differently than on a calm day.

Sometimes the intensity of your judgment has more to do with how close you are to your own limit than with whatever just drove by.

That doesn't make you fake. It just means your system has a budget.

You are not broken for caring “too much”

If you are neurodivergent, there is a good chance you have been told your whole life that you are “too sensitive,” “too intense,” or “too much” about things that feel obviously impactful to you.

Giant objects that roar through shared space and shake the air count as “impactful.” Your brain is not wrong for noticing that.

Your sensory system is not wrong for freaking out when it gets body-checked by sudden noise and motion.

Your values are not fake because your first reaction is messy and unprintable. You can be a live-and-let-live person, and still have a nervous system that goes to war with certain stimuli. You can care deeply about autonomy, and still be furious at choices that spill consequences into everyone else's day.

Those are not hypocrisy. They are tension.

And learning to live with that tension, to understand why you flare and how you want to act anyway, is a very neurodivergent kind of grown-up skill. So if your inner narrator starts shouting the next time a lifted truck bellows past, you don't have to add "horrible person" on top. You can just think, "Ah. There goes my brain, doing pattern recognition and nervous system triage again." Let the monologue play out in your head. Then let your values decide what you do with your face and your hands on the steering wheel.

You don't have to care what they drive. You only have to care how you respond, when your whole body very much does.

Those quick spikes of moral or sensory outrage are part of the same system that chases relief and novelty. In the next chapter we'll follow that energy inward to see how 'what's next' hijacks attention.

The Dopamine Scam: How My Brain Fell For "What's Next"

By the end of this chapter, you will know why 'what's next' is so sticky, and how to build motivation that does not depend on constant novelty. For most of my life, whenever someone said "enjoy the journey", my nervous system heard it as: "Just be happy while you're failing to reach the thing your brain is screaming about."

I did not enjoy the journey. I tolerated the journey. So I could maybe, finally, get to the thing.

School, work, this book, even friendships, all ran on the same glitchy script: my brain locked onto one specific "next". A goal, a fix, a notification, the next episode, the next idea. That "what's next?" feeling wrapped itself around my whole attention, like a kid pressing their face to the glass of a candy shop.

Everything else became a blurry background.

People told me I was "too future-focused" or "never satisfied." They said I should "slow down and be present" and "just enjoy the process."

Cool. Love that for them.

Meanwhile, my brain was sprinting three tabs ahead, yelling, "Yeah yeah, presence, whatever, where is the next hit of this feeling?"

It took me a long time to realize this was not a personality flaw. It was dopamine logic in a world that keeps selling one very specific, very neurotypical version of "motivation."

Dopamine, de-scienced

There is a whole complicated chemistry story here, but the part that actually helped me was stupid simple: Dopamine is not "the happy chemical." Dopamine is the anticipation chemical.

It is that leaning forward feeling. The tiny electric buzz of "almost there." The itch of "check again, check again, check again."

That feeling is not a sign you are broken. It is literally your brain doing what it evolved to do.

The scam part starts when the world around you keeps acting like dopamine = reward only when you finish.

Study hard, then you get the A. Work hard, then you get the promotion. Grind on this project for months, then you get the thing you can finally enjoy. Write that book, then become some sort of pseudo-celebrity. This is called foreshadowing by the way! Right? Right!

If your brain is wired like mine, that model falls apart fast.

My brain doesn't wait patiently for the "someday reward." It wants micro hits of "almost" every few seconds. It wants movement, not medals. It wants to feel like it's closing loops all the time.

So when TikTok, push alerts, and infinite scroll walked in like, "What if we gave you tiny almost-rewards every 0.3 seconds," my brain just shook their hand.

Of course I fell for it.

The slot machine in my pocket

I didn't sit down one day and say, “You know what my nervous system needs? A portable casino that fits in my palm.” But that is what short-form feeds feel like to me. Every flick of my thumb is a new dopamine lottery ticket. Maybe this one will be boring. Maybe this one will be mildly interesting. Maybe this one will punch me straight in the feelings.

Either way, the part of my brain that loves possibility lights up at the idea there is always one more.

The loop goes like this: You scroll, you flinch, you care. War. Disasters. Another rights rollback. A GoFundMe for basic medical care. A friend texting you from burnout, again. You scroll, you laugh, you save. You scroll, you get mad, you share.

Each of those is a mini hit of “something is happening.” Even when the feeling is bad, the anticipation system is thrilled. It gets to keep chasing what's next.

Meanwhile, your actual body? Your eyes are dry, your back hurts, your brain fog is building, you've been doing cricket feet for an hour straight, and you can't remember why you opened your phone in the first place.

I used to tell myself I was just “bad at self-control.” What helped more was admitting that these apps are very good at triggering dopamine, and that my brain is very responsive to it.

That is not a weakness. That is wiring meeting an environment designed to keep you hooked.

When "what's next?" eats "what's here?"

The real cost for me was not "guilty screen time." It was the way "what's next?" ate my ability to feel anything good about "what's here?"

I could be:

- sitting with a friend I love
- working on a project I actually chose
- doing something I know is meaningful to me

and still feel this low-grade hum of "you should be somewhere else doing something more."

Not more fun, even. Just more urgent.

Dopamine had quietly shifted from "wow, I am excited about this thing I'm doing" into "I only feel alive when I'm chasing the next thing I haven't done yet."

The second I finished something, it turned into emotional cardboard. No taste. No texture. No satisfaction.

Moments, achievements, even rest, all got vacuumed into the same hole: already done, no longer interesting.

If that's you, hear this very clearly: You are not ungrateful. You do not "lack joy." Your reward system is running on a different clock.

The world keeps telling you to soak in the moment. Your brain is getting pushed forward by a chemical that cares more about the arrow than the target.

The scam inside "just enjoy the journey"

Here is why "enjoy the journey" landed so badly for me. It always seemed to come from people who:

- could feel steady satisfaction from slow progress
- did not have a circus of notifications screaming for their attention
- were not trying to do basic life tasks with a brain set to "max sensitivity."

They talked as if the journey itself were automatically rewarding if I just adjusted my attitude. For me, the "journey" was mostly:

- confusing project instructions
- forty-five steps of invisible prep
- five false starts
- and constant internal error messages about everything I was forgetting

There was not a lot to enjoy there.

What's slowly helping me is shifting the question from: "Why can't I enjoy the whole journey as they do?" to "Where, exactly, does my brain feel dopamine along the way?"

Because there actually were parts of the process I loved. They were just not the ones school posters or productivity apps cared about.

My dopamine did not light up at "stick with it for three months." It lit up at "start the thing," "fix the problem," "figure out a clever shortcut," "share the result with someone who gets it."

Nobody had framed any of those moments as valid "reward" spots. They were treated as warm-up, or maintenance, or extras.

So I felt like I was failing the game when, really, I was playing on a different level.

Effort dopamine, not just finish-line dopamine

Somewhere between burnout, therapy, and another late-night spiral of "why am I like this," I stumbled across an idea that actually clicked: Dopamine is not only about the reward. It can come from the effort itself.

Not in a vague "love the grind" way. In a very literal "my brain feels good when it senses movement toward something that matters to me" way.

This reframed a lot.

Instead of waiting to feel okay only at the finish line, I started looking for tiny, bite-sized "effort wins" my brain could feel along the way.

Stuff like:

- "I opened the document. That's movement."
- "I set a 10-minute timer and stuck with it. That's movement."
- "I answered one hard email. That's movement."

This is not about toxic positivity. Some tasks are still boring, painful, or draining. They don't magically become fun because you rebrand them. What changed was that my brain started getting credit signals earlier and more often. Instead of "nothing counts until you submit the project," it became: "every visible nudge counts as a mini success."

Effort dopamine is basically telling your brain: "Hey, the story is not only 'done or fail.' The story is 'you are in motion, and that already matters.'"

Flow states: the anti-scam

Every so often, something grabs my attention so fully that time collapses.

You look up and hours have passed. You forgot to check your phone. You weren't chasing anything else, because your whole brain was inside the thing.

That is flow. It is when challenge and skill line up just right, and your attention gets to be single, instead of shredded.

For my dopamine system, flow is like finally getting to put all the lights on one stage instead of trying to light fifty tabs at once.

In flow, "what's next" and "what's here" actually match. The next tiny step is inside the moment you are in.

There are no sirens screaming from other rooms. There is no guilt about "you should be over there." The process starts to feel rewarding in real time, not as a moral lesson afterward.

I don't live in flow. I visit.

But even knowing that my brain is capable of that state helped. It meant I was not doomed to a lifetime of only feeling alive in short-form scrolls and last-minute crises. My dopamine could lock onto something deep and steady. It just needed the right conditions.

Tiny rebellions against the dopamine trap

I wish I could end with a clean "5-step system to fix your dopamine." That would sell so well, I'd be rich, and no one would ever hear from me again. Sadly, my brain doesn't do systems. It does experiments.

Here are a few that have helped me relate to my dopamine instead of fighting it:

- I treat my "what's next" obsession as data, not a moral failing. If I can't stop thinking about the next thing, it usually means I need more visible progress markers in what I am doing now.
- I build tasks so they have more finish lines, not one giant one. If my brain loves "done," then cool, I give it a dozen little "done" moments inside a bigger project.
- I try to get at least one flow-adjacent pocket per day. Not full cinematic flow, just 20 to 40 minutes where my phone is nowhere near me and I am doing one thing that feels like it uses my actual brain.

None of this turns me into the calm, slow-breathing person who just "enjoys the journey" on command.

What it does is give my dopamine system more places to land that are not just bright apps or future fantasies. It widens the map a bit.

You are not a broken reward machine

If your brain is always chasing the next thing, if short videos feel like gravity, if finishing something makes it instantly boring, there is nothing uniquely wrong with you.

You are living with a highly sensitive anticipation system in a world that is very eager to monetize that.

"Enjoy the journey" was not built with you in mind. Standard motivation advice was not, either.

You are allowed to build different routes to satisfaction. Routes with more checkpoints. Routes where effort actually counts. Routes where flow is not some mystical accident, just a state you know you can visit sometimes.

You don't have to kill your desire for “what’s next.” You get to aim it. At things that matter to you. At processes that give you micro-rewards, not just final grades. At lives that feel a little less like slot machines, and a little more like something your particular brain knows how to inhabit.

You are not broken. Your dopamine is just fluent in forward.

Chasing 'almost rewards' is exhausting. Over time, the sprint wears you out in a way that is not dramatic but is deeply eroding. The next chapter sits with that worn-out, gray feeling and what it means for living day to day.

The Quiet Middle: Not Suicidal, Not In Love With Living

I'm lowering the jokes here because this bit matters. If you are in immediate danger or making plans to hurt yourself, please pause and reach out to local emergency support. If the topic of death is sensitive for you, please skip this chapter. It will still be here later. You don't have to earn your safety by reading about hard things.

This chapter is for the gray middle, not planning to die, just tired of existing. There is a sentence I have carried around for years like a stone in my pocket.

If I died, would that really be so bad?

Not in a dramatic, movie-scene way. More in a bored, slightly over-it way, the same tone you might use for, "If this meeting got cancelled, would that really be so bad?"

I'm not planning my death. I'm not drawing up timelines or writing final notes. I'm just, very often, exhausted by the ongoing project of existing.

If you're still reading, I'm guessing some part of you knows that feeling. You wake up, you tick the boxes, you do the things. You work, you reply, you feed yourself enough to stay functional. You are technically "alive," but you do not really feel like you're living.

Yet somewhere in the background, there is this quiet thought: If a bus hit me tomorrow, I would be dead. I wouldn't know. I don't think there is a heaven or hell. It would all just stop. And that, honestly, sounds… fine. Maybe even peaceful.

I don't think you're supposed to say this out loud. I contemplated multiple times removing this chapter altogether just to avoid questions from family and friends who read it, because when people hear statements like this, they tend to jump straight to "You are suicidal" or "You need emergency help." Sometimes that is true. Sometimes it's not.

I hope that you are not trying to die. But it's also understandable if you just aren't impressed by life as it is currently presented to you.

This is the weird, gray, uncomfortable space I want to talk about.

Late-diagnosed, burnt out, and doing the math on existing

For me, this sits very close to late-diagnosed neurodivergent burnout.

By the time I had language for being autistic, I already had decades of being "the capable one" and "the high-functioning one" behind me. Which really meant decades of masking, people-pleasing, and grinding through sensory, social, and emotional overload because I thought that's just what life was.

On the outside, I kept checking the boxes. Good at work. Reasonably social. Not a mess on paper.

On the inside, it felt like this:

- My energy was a bank account that went negative most days
- Joy was rare, like a glitch in the system

- Everything cost something, and the "rewards" did not quite balance it out

That is the burnout feeling. Not just tired, but soul-tired. You can sleep for twelve hours and still wake up already over it. In that state, my brain starts doing a kind of strange, cold math. Life is a lot of effort. Relationships, work, housing, meals, health, just existing in a body in a world that is too loud, too bright, too much. I know that people around me get something from me being alive. They would be hurt if I died. There would be grief, loss, shock.

But if I died, I wouldn't be there to care.

I don't believe in a next phase with harps or torture. I believe in "lights out." So part of me goes: All of this effort is for a life I'm not sure I want, to avoid a death I'm not actually afraid of, so that other people get to keep me. And I am tired.

It feels cold to admit that. Selfish, even.

But it's not cruelty. It's burnout doing math with the limited energy it has left.

Not suicidal, just existentially tired

I want to draw a clear line here, because it matters.

There is a difference between:

- "I want to die."
- "I don't want to be hurt."
- "I don't want to hurt other people."
- "I'm not sure I want to keep doing this whole life thing."

They get tangled together in conversation, but inside my head, they are separate sliders. I'm not sitting here planning my death.

I'm not seeking out ways to make it happen. That is actively considering suicide, and when people are in that state, they need real, immediate support.

My thing is quieter. It sounds more like:

- I'm not afraid of death itself
- I'm afraid of pain, both mine and other people's
- I don't want to cause suffering
- I also don't really feel a strong pull toward staying alive for my own sake

So I keep living, mostly, to avoid hurting other people and to avoid experiencing suffering on the way out. I'm not terrified of being dead. I'm terrified of dying badly and leaving chaos behind. And that is what keeps me here. Not some huge, blazing love of life. More like a very reluctant sense of responsibility, mixed with a basic instinct to avoid pain.

It's not pretty. It's not inspirational. It's just, honestly, how it is.

The weird rational calm of "lights out"

If you don't believe in an afterlife, death can become oddly neutral. Not a punishment. Not a reward. Just an off switch. That "off switch" idea has always felt strangely calming to me. It turns death from a monster into more of a technical event. Eventually, my body will stop. Then I won't have to think about anything anymore. I won't be stuck in this constant stream of sensory input, social puzzles, and emotional admin.

That thought doesn't make me want to jump in front of a train. It just lets my whole body unclench a little when life feels like too much.

Because in the back of my mind, there's this quiet reassurance: I don't have to carry this forever. One day it will stop.

For neurotypical people who are deeply attached to life, that can sound horrifying. For a burnt-out neurodivergent brain, it can feel like the only non-anxious thought in the room.

When people say, "But you mean so much to us, you can't think like that," they are missing the point. I know I matter to them. I do care about that. It just doesn't always feel like enough to outweigh the constant cost of existing inside my own head. That is not a moral failure. It is a mismatch between how hard life is and how much it gives back, especially when you have spent years masking, overperforming, and ignoring your own limits.

You are not broken for thinking this

If any of this sounds like you, let me say the thing you are probably not hearing enough. You are not evil or broken for having that "If I died, would that be so bad?" thought. You are not automatically in crisis every single time your brain wanders there, either.

You might be:

- Burnt out, especially in a long-term, chronic way
- Underwhelmed by the life you are currently allowed to live
- Overwhelmed by the sensory and social cost of existing
- Deeply rational in your view of death as an end point

None of this means you should die. It also doesn't mean you have to suddenly become grateful for every sunrise and join a positivity cult. What it does mean is that your relationship with life and death is more complex than the posters on a therapist's wall.

You can not be especially afraid of death and still choose to stay alive, purely on your own terms. You can keep existing for small reasons. A person. A pet. A story you have not finished writing yet. A show you want to see the end of. Or even just to avoid hurting the people you care about.

That choice is not less real because your motivation is quiet, or complicated, or not very inspirational-quote-friendly.

It is still your choice. You are still here. That counts.

What if this is burnout, not a moral failure?

One of the most freeing thoughts for me has been: Maybe I'm not heartless. Maybe I'm just tired.

I'm tired from:

- Years of ticking boxes instead of living
- Years of feeling different without knowing why
- Years of pushing through when my brain and body were screaming for a break

When I see my "death is not scary" voice as a symptom of burnout, not proof that I am broken, it shifts something. It doesn't magically make life beautiful, but it takes away some shame.

Instead of, "What kind of person thinks like this?", it becomes: "Of course I think like this. Look at how drained I am. Look at how little space I've had to actually want things."

From that place, the work is not "learn to love life more." The work is much smaller and more practical.

- Where can I take off a mask?

- What can I stop doing that is only there to make other people comfortable?
- What is one tiny thing that makes existing feel a little less pointless? Not meaningful in a movie sense. Just… less empty.

Those are not magic fixes. They also don’t fix capitalism, or ableism, or the sensory nightmare that is most public spaces. But they are friction reducers, and when you are this tired, every bit of reduced friction matters.

Existing, even when you are not convinced

I'm not going to wrap this up with “And now I am thrilled to be alive.” That would be a lie.

I still have days where I feel like a background extra in my own life. I still have that quiet, rational voice that says, “If you died, you wouldn't know. It wouldn't bother you.”

The difference now is that I do not treat that voice like a crime. I treat it as information.

It tells me I am tired. It tells me I am undernourished in some deep, non-food way. It tells me my life, as currently arranged, asks more of me than it gives back. And instead of panicking about the thought itself, I try to adjust the conditions of my life so that existing costs a little less.

If you walk around with the same quiet sentence in your pocket, know this: You are not the only one. You are not cursed. You are not automatically about to die.

You are a person who is not afraid of death, and who is very, very tired of life as it has been so far.

That doesn't make you a monster. It makes you honest.

“GOOD” IS NOT A FEELING: A STARTER GUIDE FOR BLURRY EMOTIONS

Recently, my therapist ruined my life in a very specific, useful way. She asked me how I felt after something nice happened, and I said, “Yeah, it felt good.” She nodded, paused, then said, “You know good isn’t an emotion, right?”

I thought to myself, "Excuse me? I didn't know you were the emotion police now!"

By the time we get here, we're in that quiet middle: not in crisis, not okay, just flat. The kind of tired where everything gets filed under “fine” because reaching for more precise language feels like too much effort.

For a long time, "good" was my all-purpose label for every inner state. Tired but proud? That became "good." Relieved but a little scared? Also "good".

If you have trouble naming your feelings, you might know this move. Some people call it alexithymia. It means emotions can be hard to identify. You have two or three words you use for everything inside you. Maybe good, bad, fine, and stressed. That is the whole emotional menu.

Most people think that means nothing is happening up there in the brain. But there's actually a lot happening. It is blurry and unlabeled, like a grocery bag full of mystery food with the labels torn off.

My therapist asking "what does good actually mean?" was the moment I realized I didn't know how to answer. Not because there was nothing there, but because I didn't have the language or the habits to sort it out. That is where the idea of practicing emotions came in for me. Not feeling them perfectly. Not naming them instantly.

Practicing.

The feelings wheel as training wheels

So now I have a feelings wheel.

If you've never seen one, it is a circle with basic emotions in the middle and more specific ones around the edges. Kind of like a color wheel, but for your insides. For me, it has become less of a poster and more of a translation device. It's what I reach for when my brain says "good" or "bad" and refuses to be more specific.

A typical moment looks like this: Something happens. I get that vague sense of "good." Instead of stopping there, I pull up the wheel and start poking around like I'm filling out a multiple-choice test I didn't study for. Does this "good" feel more like relief or joy? More like proud or grateful? Is there calm in it, or excitement, or both?

It's clumsy. I'm often guessing. Sometimes I pick a word and it feels completely wrong five minutes later. But that's the whole point. I'm not trying to be a human emotion scanner. I'm trying to build a habit of looking closer.

If you are alexithymic, this part matters. People often tell us to "just feel it in your body." That can be helpful, but if your ability to notice body signals is weaker or just works differently, you might only feel something like 'vague buzzing' or 'my stomach is doing something,' and not much else. So the feelings wheel becomes a kind of ladder. You start from the vague thing, then climb toward something slightly more specific. You don't need to find the perfect word. You just need to get one step closer to something other than "good."

Why I want to practice sadness on purpose

The other emotion I am trying to practice is sadness. That one surprised me. I have had some frustrating things happen recently that made me feel sad. At least, I think it's sadness. The old me would have called it "annoyed" or "tired" or "whatever." Anything but sad.

Sadness used to feel like a trap. If I stepped into it, I would get stuck. If I admitted I was sad, it might mean I was weak or dramatic, or that I needed something from people that I didn't know how to ask for. Even more so, sadness as a guy can sometimes be viewed negatively in a variety of ways.

But my gut keeps telling me, while I watch other people handle their own hard things, that feeling sadness might actually be good for us. Not fun. Not pleasant. More like… human. I see people cry, or say "I am really sad about this," and instead of falling apart forever, they seem more real. More connected. Sometimes even softer and kinder with themselves after.

I look at that and think, "Okay, whatever that is, I want to learn it."

So I decided to treat sadness like a skill I'm weak in, not a defect in my wiring. If I can practice writing. If I can practice a new hobby. I can practice sadness.

What practicing sadness actually looks like

Practicing an emotion sounds a bit abstract, so let me try to make it concrete.

When something frustrating or disappointing happens now, my old reflexes still show up. Minimize it. Reframe it. Move on. Call it “fine” or “just tired.” What I'm trying to do now is catch that reflex and interrupt it. Instead of skipping ahead, I pause long enough to ask, “Could this be sadness?”

That's it. Not very impressive. Not cinematic. Just a tiny question inside my head.

If the answer feels like “maybe,” I go to the feelings wheel again. I look at the sadness slice and see words that are usually strangers to me. Lonely. Disappointed. Hurt. Hopeless. Powerless. I test them out one by one, like trying keys in a lock.

“Is this disappointed?” “Is this lonely?” “Is this hurt?”

Sometimes I land on one that clicks, and it feels like I can relax with confidence for just one moment. Like, “Oh. That's what this is.” Not fixed, not solved, but identified.

Sometimes nothing fits. When that happens, I still practice by saying to myself, “Okay, I think I'm some sad, even if I do not know which kind. That is allowed.” It sounds small, but for me, it's huge. Because to even think “I am sad” is a different story than “I am overreacting” or “I am being weird” or “this shouldn't bother me.”

The other thing I'm experimenting with is letting sadness sit with me for a bit.

Instead of rushing to “it is fine” or “I should be grateful,” I try to sit with it. Maybe that looks like lying on the bed, staring at the ceiling, and letting myself feel heavy for ten minutes. Perhaps it's writing down one sentence about why it hurts, which then eventually becomes a whole chapter in a book.

I don't always succeed. Sometimes I bail out and distract myself. Sometimes I get annoyed at the whole process and shut down.

But even then, I'm at least aware that I bailed out of sadness. That is still data. It is still practice.

When you do not know you are alexithymic

Part of why I wanted to write about this is for the people who do not yet have the word alexithymia, but live the reality of it.

If you have spent your life saying "good," "bad," and "fine" and secretly feeling like everyone else got an internal user manual you missed, you are not alone.

You might not have grown up thinking, "I have alexithymia." You might have grown up thinking things like:

- "I am just not emotional"
- "I overreact, then shut down, and I don't understand why"
- "I feel things too intensely, but I can't explain them"
- "I only realize how I felt about something three days later"

Practicing emotions is not about turning yourself into a Hallmark card. It is not about having poetic language for every flicker of your inner world. It is about noticing that there is an inner world. That it is not empty. That it might even be rich, but unlabeled. And then deciding to build some labels, one clumsy repetition at a time.

I think a lot of us carry quiet shame around this. We assume that if we cannot easily name or feel our emotions, we are less human.

Or less kind. Or less capable of real connection. What I keep learning is that confusion is not the same thing as coldness.

Not having language for feelings is not the same thing as not having feelings.

The "something more" you can learn

My therapist telling me "good is not an emotion" didn't magically fix anything. I didn't log off of that session, suddenly fluent in my inner life.

What it did, though, was open a door.

It told me there was more detail available than I had ever been taught to look for. It told me that my "good" might sometimes be relief, or pride, or safety, or joy, or peace. That my "bad" might sometimes be sadness, or fear, or shame, or anger.

That there is something more I can learn.

If you see yourself in any of this, that is the main thing I want you to leave with. Not "I am broken." Not "I am way behind everyone else." Just this: there is more granularity available than you have right now. You can practice toward it. Slowly. Imperfectly. Awkwardly. Like any other skill.

You can:

- Use tools like the feelings wheel as training wheels, not as a test
- Pick one emotion, like sadness, and experiment with spotting it more often
- Let yourself be wrong, then try again, without deciding that being wrong means you are hopeless

I'm nowhere near "good" at this yet. Ironically, that is the wrong word again. I'm not polished at it. I'm not consistent. What I am is curious. Yes, maybe I'm curious because my therapist is forcing me to, but I'm curious nonetheless. I'm curious enough to keep asking what "good" actually means. Curious enough to let myself be sad on purpose sometimes, because I suspect it might grow my humanity, not shrink it.

If you are alexithymic, or suspect you might be, curiosity might be the most important emotion-adjacent thing you can practice. It is the one thing that keeps you turning toward your inner world instead of away from it. You may not yet know the names for what you feel. You may not feel them correctly.

That is okay.

You can still learn. There is more in you than "good" and "bad." And it's worth getting to know.

When you can tell the difference between relief and joy, you also notice how you sound. Naming feelings helps you track whether your delivery matches your intent. Next we will look at tone: how your voice can betray your intentions and what to do about it.

YOUR TONE IS TRASH (AND OTHER THINGS NO ONE TELLS YOU)

I'm so tired of getting smacked around by other people's tone.

Not their words, but their tone. This isn't a character flaw on their part. It's a skills gap plus nervous system stuff.

You probably know this feeling. You walk into a conversation with good intentions, or at least neutral ones. You say something reasonable. Maybe you even took time to phrase it carefully. Then the other person responds, and the content is technically fine, but the way they say it lands like a slap.

It feels hostile. Or contemptuous. Or so heavy with irritation that your nervous system goes straight into alert mode.

Meanwhile, everyone around you seems to think things are fine. “They were just explaining.” “You're being too sensitive.” “You know they didn't mean it like that.”

Cool. Great. Love that for us.

This is the space I want to sit in with you. The messy overlap where:

- Some neurodivergent people are hyper-attuned to tone and feel every sharp edge.
- Some neurodivergent people do not notice how their delivery is landing and think people are mad at their ideas when, in fact, people are just exhausted by the way they talk.
- And a lot of us are getting hurt and confused in the middle, then blaming ourselves.

So let's talk about it. Let's drag tone out into the light, poke at it a bit, and be honest about what's happening, especially in neurodivergent communication.

Because if people keep telling you your tone is a problem, or you keep noticing that others pull away from you, you might not be cursed or misunderstood or "too honest. I know this sounds harsh, but your tone might just be trash. And you might not be noticing it.

Yet.

That is fixable.

What I mean when I say "your tone is trash"

When I say "your tone is trash," I'm not calling you trash.

I am talking about that specific pattern where the content of what you say is not the issue, but the delivery is so loaded that it wrecks the entire interaction.

You say something like, "Well, obviously you should have done it this way," with that sharp, cutting edge in your voice. Or you respond to someone's vulnerable share with a flat, cold "Okay." Or you talk to people in a way that sounds like a tired teacher scolding a class that keeps failing the same test.

And then you're surprised when people react badly. You think they're mad at your opinion. So you dig in. You defend the logic. You explain why you're not actually wrong. What you can't hear, though, is that people aren't reacting to a debate. They're reacting to the emotional signal you broadcast with your tone.

If all you're tuned into is, "Were my words correct?" you're going to miss that what came out of your mouth was not "information." It was disgust. Or contempt. Or exhaustion with this topic, which the other person understandably hears as exhaustion with them.

This is especially brutal when you have good intentions. You feel like you're trying to help, or clarify, or solve something, and what people experience is being talked down to, shut down, or dismissed.

That gap, between intention and impact, lives mostly in tone.

Neurodivergent brains and tone: different settings, same mess

Let's go back to the mixing-board analogy I keep referring to. I think of tone like volume knobs on that mixing board. Think of knobs like sarcasm, pitch, or bluntness; each one you can turn up or down.

Most people grow up with their "tone board" shaped by trial and error in social life. They get feedback, they adjust. They mess up, but they more or less learn which sliders to keep low and which ones to push up around different people.

Neurodivergent people often have those sliders set to weird levels, and the learning process looks very different.

Some of us have:

- The “detective mode” slider turned up to max. We track micro-shifts in tone, tiny pauses, and changes in pitch. We notice tone like other people notice flashing lights.
- The “self-monitoring” slider turned way down. We struggle to hear our own tone as others hear it, or to adjust quickly enough in real time.
- The “emotion intensity” slider is set sky high. So any irritation or anxiety that bumps our tone comes out much stronger than we think.
- The “context guess” slider is all over the place. We misread someone’s neutral tone as anger, or we miss that our joking tone is landing as cruel.

Not every neurodivergent person has the same pattern. As we've shared before, this isn't a “one type of autistic” thing or a “one type of ADHD” thing. It's more like there are spectrums inside the spectrum, and tone is one of them.

Some of us are oversensitive to others' tone and undersensitive to our own.

Some of us are brutally literal. We listen mostly to content, not tone, so we cannot understand what people are upset about when our words make sense.

And some of us are doing both at once. Hyper-attuned to other people’s tone. Half-deaf to our own.

That is a fun combo.

Being on the receiving end of shitty tone

Let me linger on this one, because it's the part that hurts the most.

You go into a conversation with good intentions. You're trying to commit to something, or fix something, or just be honest. You are already using a lot of energy to be careful, to not come across as rude, to manage your own tone as best you can.

Then the other person responds in a way that feels like:

- They are annoyed you even asked
- They think you're stupid for not already knowing
- They are barely tolerating you

Their words might be totally reasonable. “Well, that is not quite right, here is how it works.” Or “You could have done this instead.” Or “I already told you that.”

Fine. Great. On paper, that looks like information.

But the way they say it hits like, “Obviously, idiot.” Or, “You are a burden, and I am tired of you.” Or, “Why are you still not getting this? What is wrong with you?”

You feel the impact in your body. Tightness in your chest. A drop in your stomach. Heat in your face. Anger, shame, or that heavy, sinking “Why do I even bother?” feeling. You might second-guess yourself. You might tell yourself you are overreacting. You might try to shrug it off. But the tension sits there. And after a while, it builds into resentment.

Because it is not one moment. It is a pattern.

The pattern of being around someone whose tone is always a little bit cruel, or a little bit disgusted, or permanently impatient. They don't scream at you. They don't swear at you. They just talk in a way that makes your nervous system feel like it's being graded and failed all day.

And no one around you seems to notice.

That mismatch is gaslighting-adjacent, even if no one intends it that way. You feel something real. Other people don't see it. You start to doubt your senses. Sometimes, as neurodivergent people, we are misreading things. That happens. Our pattern recognition gets weird. Our past experiences color what we hear.

But sometimes, we are picking up something very real that others have tuned out. We are tracking those tone sliders in vivid detail, while everyone else just hears "normal conversation."

It is not overreacting to name that.

The pain of having good intentions

Here is where this gets really tangled.

Often, the person with the harsh tone doesn't think they're being harsh. They believe they're being clear. Or helpful. Or simply correct.

They are thinking about:

- The information they want to deliver
- The mistake they want to point out
- The logic they want to defend

They are not thinking about the emotional layer that rides on top of their words. They probably have a long history of people "not getting" their intent, so by now they are defensive about it.

"I'm just saying the truth."

"If you can't handle honesty, that's your problem."

"I'm tired of having to sugar-coat everything."

Behind that, there is often pain. Years of being misunderstood. Years of masking, of being told to "say it nicer," of having their bluntness treated like a character flaw.

So when someone says, "Your tone is a problem," they hear, "Your existence is a problem." And they fight it. I have empathy for that. I really do. I know how it feels to be punished for how your brain naturally expresses itself. To be told that "how you talk" is wrong when you are just trying to be honest.

But at some point, if multiple people have told you that your tone feels awful, or if you notice that people pull away from you, or get defensive around you, or stop bringing you things, you have to pause. It's not always the world being fragile. Sometimes, your tone is hitting people like a truck.

Even if you don't mean it that way.

If people keep telling you about your tone, maybe listen

This is the pointed part.

If people in your life keep saying things like:

- "You don't seem to like me"
- "You always sound mad"
- "I feel like you're talking down to me"
- "Your tone is really harsh"

Or, they stop saying it, and instead, you notice that:

- People avoid asking you questions
- Friends share less with you

- Conversations with you feel shorter, colder, or more "business only"
- People tell other people they are scared of your reactions

You need to take that seriously.

Not because you are a monster. Not because your actual feelings are wrong. But because impact matters, and tone is where impact lives. If you keep hearing, "Your tone is a problem," and your automatic response is, "No it isn't, you are just sensitive," you are basically saying, "My internal experience is more real than your external one."

That is the same thing that has hurt you your whole life, just flipped.

People ignoring what you say you are feeling. People insisting that their read on you is more accurate than your own. You know how horrible that is.

So when someone tells you, "The way you are speaking to me feels awful," that is not the time to disappear into logic debates about message versus method. That is the time to say, inside your own head if nothing else, "Okay. Something about my tone is not landing. I do not fully hear it. But it is real for them. So it is real enough."

Why tone is so hard for neurodivergent people

I want to be clear that this is not a pure "personal failing" thing.

Tone is hard because:

- Our sensory and emotional systems are wired differently. What feels neutral to us might feel intense to others, or the reverse.

- Many of us didn't get accurate feedback growing up. We got yelled at for things we didn't understand, or praised for masking, not for authentic communication.
- We may use words as our main navigation tool, and be under-practiced at tracking the nonverbal side of interaction.
- We can be working with chronic overload. When you're already stressed, your tone shifts without your conscious input.

On top of that, neurodivergent culture sometimes celebrates bluntness in a way that quietly erases impact. We talk about "brutal honesty," or "just say what you mean," like that solves everything. Honesty is important. Clear speech is important. Directness can be a relief. But there is a difference between direct and hostile. Between "I disagree with you" and "I can't hide my contempt for you."

Tone is not about being fake or sugar-coating.

It's about translating your intent into something other humans can actually receive.

Listening to yourself without melting

If you suspect your tone might be a problem, or you have been told that it is, you don't have to turn into a smiling customer service robot. You don't have to erase your anger or your annoyance. But you do have to start paying attention.

That might look like:

- Noticing patterns. For example, "Whenever I feel slightly irritated, my voice goes flat and sharp. People hear that as rage, even when I feel only mildly annoyed."

- Trying to hear your own words from the outside. You might play back a conversation in your head and ask yourself, not "Was I right?" but "If someone talked to me in that tone, how would I feel?"
- Remembering that your default tone is not neutral. It's just familiar to you. Other people are not "wrong" for hearing things you don't feel.

You can also give yourself reminders. When you feel the urge to correct someone, you can pause and ask, "Do I want to help, or do I want to vent my frustration at their mistake?" Both are valid feelings. Only one is likely to help the relationship. Sometimes, the compassionate move is not to say the thing at all. Sometimes, it's to soften your entry. "Okay, let me try to explain it a different way," lands very differently than, "We already went over this."

Again, this is not about being fake. It's about not confusing your momentary irritation with moral truth.

For the hyper-attuned among us

If you're the one who hears every sharp edge, every little sigh, every hint of sarcasm that isn't supposed to be there, I see you. I am you.

You are not wrong for noticing. Your sensory and emotional radar might be picking up things that other people have learned to ignore. Your sensitivity is not a character flaw. It is data. But it is also exhausting, and it can get you caught in loops of hurt.

There are two tricky truths here:

1. Sometimes, your read is absolutely correct. Their tone is contemptuous. It is cruel. Other people have just normalized it.

2. Sometimes, your nervous system is firing old alarms. A neutral comment lands like an attack because it sounds like past attacks.

You don't have to decide which it is in the moment. You can step back and say to yourself, "Regardless of intent, this does not feel good." That is enough to act on. You get to decide how close you want to be to people whose default tone leaves you feeling small or stupid.

You also get to communicate about impact without litigating intent. "You might not mean it this way, but when you talk to me in that tone, I shut down." If they're willing to hear that, great. If they're not, that is also information.

Tone, accountability, and care

Tone is where accountability and care meet.

If you know your tone tends to come out sharp, you have a responsibility to factor that in. Not because you're wrong for having feelings, but because communication is a two-way thing. If you know you are hyper-attuned to tone, you also have a responsibility to care for yourself and not make yourself stay in spaces that feel like a constant low-level attack.

This is not about blaming neurodivergent people for being "bad at communication." It is about being honest that our differences in tone processing can cause real harm, even when no one means to hurt anyone.

Being neurodivergent doesn't give you a free pass to talk to people however you like and then blame them for reacting. It also doesn't mean you have to tolerate shitty tone from others, just because they are neurodivergent too, or because "that is just how they are."

We can do better for each other. We can be more curious about how our tone lands. We can believe people when they tell us that something feels bad, even if we can't hear it yet. We can hold both: "My brain is wired this way," and "I am still responsible for how my words land."

The quiet ask

So here's my quiet ask, especially if you've been told repeatedly that your tone comes across as harsh, cold, or mean.

Please, pay attention.

When someone flinches, pauses, or goes distant, don't just double down on the logic of what you were saying. Take a breath. Ask yourself what your voice might sound like from where they are standing. If people keep pulling away from you, it's not always because they are weak. Sometimes they are tired of being treated like a problem you are trying to solve.

And if you are the one who hears too much, feels too much, and walks away from conversations wondering why no one else seems to notice how painful they are, you are not crazy. You are just tuned in a different way. You are allowed to trust that. You are allowed to say, "This tone is not okay for me." You are allowed to leave.

Somewhere between those two positions, the over-sharp and the over-exposed, there is a space where we actually hear each other.

That is where I want us to be. Not perfect. Not scripted. And if your tone is trash, you can clean it up. You are allowed to learn how.

Tone matters most where we rely on small signals to keep a friendship alive. In the next chapter, we will take tone out of the abstract and into your texts, check-ins, and the friendships you keep fixing.

Always The One Who Texts First: A Neurodivergent Friendship Survival Guide

If you stopped, would this friendship even exist? By the time you hit this chapter, you probably have at least a few people in your life already. Some you love, some you are not sure about, some you are clinging to out of habit and history. This chapter is mostly about those existing connections and what it is like to maintain them with a brain that has patchy social batteries and a threat radar that's always two steps ahead.

You can adore people, feel deeply connected to them, and still spend three weeks drafting a two-line text in your head. You can know, logically, they like me, and still spiral when their reply energy changes. You can be the one who is always reaching out, yet forget to reply for days.

Welcome to the neurodivergent friendship settings menu.

"Why am I always the one reaching out?"

Let's start with that stingy-feeling one.

You look at your chats, and it feels like the same pattern every time. You start the conversation. You suggest the hangout. You send the “hey, how are you?” check-in. Your brain quietly whispers, "If I stopped, would this friendship even exist?"

Two things are usually happening at once.

First, your neurodivergent brain is tracking effort like a bloodhound. You notice who messages, how often, and how fast. That pattern-detection is part of how you survive the chaos. The downside is that friendship can start to feel like a spreadsheet where you are always in the red.

Second, many neurodivergent folks are really good at emotional work. Reading tone. Remembering what people are dealing with. Anticipating needs. We get slotted into the role of the one who reaches out, partly because we genuinely care, and partly because people get used to us doing it.

Both are true.

So yes, sometimes you are doing too much friendship labor. And also, you may be doing more visible labor because your brain is built to notice when the connection is thinning and throws you a “fix it now” alert.

That alert feels like anxiety. It sounds like, If you don’t start this chat, they’ll forget you exist. So you hit send, again.

A tiny reframe. Reaching out first doesn't automatically mean they don’t care. It often means:

- You are more sensitive to gaps in contact
- You have higher social anxiety, so you try to “prevent” rejection by staying present
- You grew up feeling responsible for keeping relationships alive, so your default is “if it dies, it’s my fault”

That pattern is real. It is also learned. Which means we can start messing with it.

A "settings tweak" you can try. You don't have to stop reaching out suddenly. That will freak your nervous system out. Instead, treat it like an experiment.

Pick one lower-stakes friend, the kind who makes you feel good when you do talk. Then:

- Reach out like normal
- After that, pause. Give it a slightly longer gap than usual before you message again
- Let yourself notice what your brain screams at you

You are not testing if they secretly hate you. You are testing what your brain does when you are not the default initiator.

Then you get to choose, on purpose, when you want to reach out, instead of doing it because your panic is holding the phone.

"Do they actually like me, or am I annoying them?"

You know they like you. You have history, jokes, and shared chaos. But then they reply a bit shorter than usual, take longer than normal, or use a slightly colder emoji, and your whole nervous system stands up and salutes.

Suddenly it's: Did I say something wrong? Are they mad? Did I overshare? Are they bored of me? Should I apologize for existing?

For neurodivergent brains, small changes feel like huge signals. You are tuned to inconsistencies. If "Tuesday Friend" usually sends voice notes and then one day sends "k cool", it sets off the same alarm as someone yelling at you. Your body reacts first. Your logic shows up later, if at all.

The important bit: this alarm is about safety, not truth.

Your brain is doing pattern math: "Different = danger." It is not checking context like, "They might just be tired" or "They might be at work." It just fires.

A quick reality-check script (for your own head)

Next time your brain screams, run this internal script:

- "Something feels off. That doesn't mean I did something wrong."
- "Their reply changed. There are ten possible reasons. 'They hate me now' is one option, not the only one."
- "If they were actually angry, would they usually say something or go quiet? What is our actual pattern?"

You are not gaslighting yourself. You are giving your nervous system more options than panic.

A low-spoons message you can send

If the anxiety will not calm down and it is a close enough friend, you can do a light check-in that doesn't treat them like a mind reader.

Something like: "Hey, my brain is being weird about texts today, so I just want to check I didn't say something off earlier. Totally ok if you're just low energy, I just know my head loves to invent problems."

You're doing three things here. You're naming that your brain is doing A Thing. You're giving them context, "I know you might just be tired." You are keeping it low drama, so they are not forced to drop everything to reassure you.

If they do have an issue, this opens the door gently. If they don't, it gives them a chance to say, "Oh no, I'm just cooked, you're fine."

Either way, you're not alone in your own private courtroom.

"I love people. I'm just so tired. Help!"

This is the exhausting part.

You know friendship is good for you. You know you feel more human when you are connected. At the same time, maintaining those friendships can feel like an extra job that you're constantly behind on.

Neurodivergent friendship fatigue isn't just "introvert needs alone time." It's things like: You spend half an hour drafting a message in your head, then forget to actually send it. Now you feel guilty. The guilt makes it harder to reply. The harder it feels, the more you avoid it. Suddenly, it's been three weeks, and replying needs a paragraph of apology to exist.

Or you finally have energy to see people, you hang out, it's great, and then you need three days of recovery where the idea of any social contact feels heavy. Your brain whispers, You're bad at this. Other adults can just… keep up.

No. You are not bad at this. You are running friendship on a spiky battery.

Adjusting friendship expectations (without ghosting everyone)

Part of this is internal. You need your own settings for what friendship looks like on your operating system.

For example:

- “I am a person who replies slowly. That's not a moral failure. I can still be a good friend.”
- “My best friendships can survive silence. If they can't, that tells me something about the match, not my worth.”
- “I need low-pressure ways to stay present. That is allowed.”

Then there is the external part, which is scary but very freeing: telling people what your settings actually are. You don't need to give them a TED Talk. A single line can change the whole vibe.

A few scripts you can steal, adapt, and pretend you made up:

- “I’m really glad we’re friends. I’m also slow and patchy on texts, even with people I adore. Just know silence from me is always ‘brain is full’, never ‘go away’.”
- “I’m the kind of person who disappears into my own life and then pops back up like nothing happened. If that ever stresses you, tell me, and we can figure out a version that works for both of us.”
- “Low maintenance friendship is my love language. I’m not a daily chatter, but I will absolutely show up when it matters.”

You are not apologizing for existing. You are setting expectations so your friendships can work with your actual brain, rather than fight it.

Choosing “the friends that make us feel the best”

Some people may make you feel more human than others. When you talk to them, your nervous system settles. You laugh more easily. You feel less like you are performing as the “acceptable friend” character and more like you are just… there.

These are high-value friendships. Not in a cold way. In a "my brain actually rests here" way.

If you are going to spend limited social energy anywhere, start there.

It's absolutely valid to be "the one who reaches out first" more often with those people, because the return on that effort is higher. The problem is not that you initiate. The problem is when you initiate with everyone, including people who leave you drained, and then blame yourself for being tired.

So, a gentle filter you can run:

- After I talk to this person, do I feel more like myself or less?
- Do I come away calmer, or more confused and self-doubting?
- When I think about messaging them, does my body tense up or soften?

If someone consistently leaves you feeling small, anxious, or like you have to win their attention, it's ok for that friendship to move to a lighter tier. Less energy. Less checking your phone for their approval.

Save your initiator energy for the people who actually make your nervous system feel good.

You are not a bad friend. You are a different model.

Here is the thing your brain keeps skipping: most neurodivergent people are already working twice as hard internally as anyone around them realizes.

You care about your friends. You think about them when you are not talking. You replay conversations to understand what they needed. You feel guilty when you vanish, even if you were simply surviving your own life.

That care is real. It counts.

Neurodivergent friendship isn't about forcing yourself into the "always responsive, never anxious, never tired" mold. It's about letting yourself have the settings you already have, then building friendships that can live inside them.

You are allowed to:

- Be the one who reaches out more and still want effort in return
- Ask for reassurance without treating yourself like a burden
- Love people deeply and guard your energy like it is rare metal

Your brain is not running friendship on hard mode because you are defective. It's running on hard mode because it was never given a user manual.

So consider this your first draft of that manual. Now you get to keep tweaking the settings.

If your current friendships still drain you after trying these tweaks, the next chapter will help you spot the people and places that actually calm your system.

How To Recognize Your People (Even If You Can't Name The Feeling)

The previous chapter was about surviving the friendships you're already in, and shifting the ones that are quietly draining you. This chapter is about something different and much rarer, especially for neurodivergent brains that have spent years masking. That is, how to notice the people and spaces where your system actually relaxes, even if you can't yet name the feeling or explain why it is safer.

Some nights, my whole life is a Discord call that nobody is really on.

You know the ones. A few names in the corner. Maybe someone is muted and playing a game. Someone else walked away to make food. There are long stretches where nobody talks.

And somehow, that quiet rectangle of other people's presence is the safest place on earth.

This is a love letter to that feeling. To the quiet, strange, deeply autistic revolution of group calls. The way people like us build friendships that don't look like a TV show, but still hold our whole nervous system together.

This is also a small guide for anyone who has not yet found their people. Because your friendship doesn't have to look "normal" to be real.

It just has to hold.

What safety sounds like when nobody is talking

For a long time, I thought "friend time" meant constant engagement.

Talking. Laughing. Reacting fast. Keeping the vibe up. Which, if you're autistic, socially tired, or running on three spoons and a trauma brain, is… not great.

The group call taught me another model. Sometimes love looks like:

- Your friend breathing on the other end of a mic, playing Pressure Washing Simulator
- Someone typing "brb rice cake time" and not explaining further
- A shared silence that is not a test you are failing

The call is just on. You can drop in, drop out, unmute for five seconds to say "hey, look at this meme," then disappear again. It's not a performing friendship. It's co-existing in real time.

For a nervous system that's used to masking, guessing, and reading ten levels of hidden rules, that kind of low-pressure presence is a miracle. It tells your body, "You can stay as you are. These people will still be here."

It becomes the spine of your social life. Not the fancy, impressive part. The quiet structure that lets everything else move.

Autistic friendship is not broken, it is custom

If you grow up watching shows where friends burst into each other's apartments, talk for hours, and always know the right thing to say, it's easy to feel defective. You sit in a call and think, "We haven't spoken in twenty minutes. Does this count?" You spend a week not texting back and think, "I have failed the friendship exam."

There is a story that "real friendship" looks like:

- Constant talking
- Fast emotional check-ins
- Eye contact and deep sharing on a schedule

Which is funny, because our friendships often look like:

- Sending five memes instead of "How are you?"
- Parallel play on a call for three hours
- Disappearing for days or weeks, then coming back like, "So anyway, here is my Minecraft cow farm and also my feelings."

This is not a downgrade. It's a different operating system.

Autistic friendship tends to be:

- Intense, but not always frequent
- Honest, but sometimes delayed
- Steady, even when it looks quiet from the outside

You might not talk every day, but when something hits, you know who to ping. You might not hug much (or ever) in person, but you will sit with someone online while they fall apart at 2 a.m.

It counts. Your way of doing friendship is real and valid, even if it would confuse a sitcom writer.

A tiny alexithymia interlude

Now for the little psychoeducation cameo, since this book is also about education and not just vibes.

A quick introduction in case you skipped the earlier chapter on alexithymia. We'll get back into the friends-talk, but this context is helpful. Alexithymia is a fancy word for "my feelings are there, but the labeling system is garbage." A lot of autistic people have it. Some ADHD and trauma folks do too.

If emotions were tabs in a browser, a neurotypical person might see clear labels like "sad," "angry," "tired."

For us, it is more like:

- 37 tabs open
- Audio playing from somewhere
- And the only thing you can read is "GENERALIZED BADNESS (UNSPECIFIED)."

So when a friend asks, "How are you feeling?" your internal answer might honestly be, "I have no idea." Not because you don't care. But because your brain doesn't translate body-noise into words very fast.

This is where text channels and quiet calls are weirdly perfect. You can sit with yourself long enough to decode. Sometimes it looks like:

- Noticing, "Okay, my chest is tight, and I keep doomscrolling"
- Typing, "I think I'm maybe stressed?" into the chat

- Having a friend respond, “Yeah, that sounds like anxiety. Want to sit in a call and do nothing together?”

You don't need a beautiful speech. You just need one small signal that says, “I think something is off.” Other people can help you name the rest.

That is part of what the group call spine does. It gives you a place to bring your scrambled feelings, even if they're still in beta.

The “mild panic” of being truly seen

There is a special kind of terror that arrives when people actually get you. Not the version you have polished for public. The real, messy, stimmy, forgetful, hyperfixated you.

If you're used to masking, you might be running a quiet background program called “keep everyone from seeing the full disaster.” You shape your reactions, hide your overloads, laugh things off. You stay three steps ahead of rejection.

Then one day, you look up, and you're in a group call with people who:

- Remember your favorite things
- Notice when you go quiet
- Don't treat your autistic traits as a problem to fix

And your body goes, “Oh no. Oh no, this is real. I could actually lose this.” The feeling is not just joy. It is gratitude with a side of fear. You find yourself thinking, “I don't know what I did to deserve this friendship.” You scroll through old chat logs like they are sacred texts. You feel mildly panicked that there is no way to ever repay it.

That panic is a sign that this matters. It is not proof that you are unworthy. It is proof that you have finally landed somewhere that feels like home.

For the ones who have not found their people yet

If you are reading this without a Joannie, a Maddy, or an "always-on" Discord crew, I want to say something very clear.

There is nothing wrong with you. You are not late. You are not broken. You are not "too weird" for friendship.

Sometimes it just means:

- You haven't been around enough of your kind of weird yet
- You're still stuck in spaces where you have to perform too hard
- People don't understand that quiet or inconsistent contact can still mean you care

Internet spaces, fandoms, small Discord servers, niche group chats, game guilds, special interest servers, all of these can be hunting grounds for the kind of people who will happily sit in a call and say nothing with you for three hours.

Your eventual friendships might not:

- Hang out in person every week
- Remember every birthday
- Look impressive on Instagram

They might instead:

- Send you a link to a four-hour video essay and say, "This reminded me of you."
- Sit with you on a silent call while you clean your room
- Accept that sometimes you fall off the map, then welcome you back with a "hey, glad you are alive."

That still counts as real love. You are allowed to want it. You are allowed to wait for it. You are allowed to build it slowly.

The spine you are allowed to keep

When I think about friendship now, I don't picture crowded parties or constant chatter.

I picture a vertical list of usernames, glowing green. I picture a call that has been open since noon. I picture someone crunching on rice cakes on the other side of a headset while we both do our own thing.

Group calls are not a small, silly habit. For many of us, they are infrastructure. They hold our days in place. They carry the weight our nervous systems cannot carry alone.

If you have people like that, it's okay to be a little scared and a lot grateful. If you don't have them yet, it's okay to want them and to keep trying.

Your friendship doesn't have to look like anyone else's.

It just has to feel like this in your body: I can be here as I am. I am not too much. I am not not-enough. I am held, even in the quiet.

That is the whole point of the spine. It is there, even when nobody is talking.

Once you notice where your system relaxes, you will also notice how you show up in those spaces, and why you sometimes laugh when you hurt. That translation is what we cover next.

If I'm Laughing, Something Hurts: Neurodivergent Feelings In Translation

You know that feeling where your mouth starts laughing, and the rest of you is like, "What are we doing? This is a funeral!"

Yeah. That.

This is about that weird split. The one where you care a lot, your body does something that looks cold or "off," and then you either get side-eyed or you spiral about being a terrible person.

You're not a terrible person. You're just a nervous system trying its best in a loud world.

We're going to name what is actually going on, in plain language:

- Emotional armor
- Alexithymia (feelings with the labels rubbed off)
- How to support people like us, including how to support yourself

If you are neurotypical and confused already, you're welcome here too. I will flag little translations for you as we go.

Emotional armor and why you laugh when things hurt

First thing to understand: your laugh is often not about "I think this is funny." It is an automatic shield. It is the sound your body makes instead of saying, "I'm uncomfortable," or "That hurt," or "Please stop," especially if you were never taught how to say those out loud.

Sometimes your brain hits a feeling that is too big, too sharp, or just too much for the situation. Instead of letting you crumble on the spot, it throws up a joke, or a smirk, or that weird little laugh that sounds wrong even to you.

That is emotional armor.

It is like your system saying, "We are not doing a full meltdown in this grocery store aisle, thanks."

For a lot of neurodivergent people, that armor has been trained over years. Maybe you got punished for "overreacting." Maybe you were told you were "too sensitive," "too dramatic," or that your feelings made everything harder for everyone else. So your brain got very, very good at locking things down in public and even in private.

Sometimes the armor shows up as:

- Laughing at serious news
- Making a joke right after you say something painful
- Smiling during a story about trauma
- Sounding flat or casual when you talk about something that is actually huge

From the outside, people can read that as "you don't care." Inside, you might feel a mix of panic, shame, and "why am I like this?"

If you're neurotypical and watching this, the translation is: What you are seeing is not a lack of caring. It is a flood of caring that has overloaded the system and flipped the safety switch.

That "wrong time" laugh is not a moral failure. It is a stress response.

Alexithymia: Feelings with the labels rubbed off

Emotional armor is one piece. Another common piece is alexithymia.

As a quick reminder, in case you skipped the earlier chapter, alexithymia means: you have feelings, you just can't easily tell what they are or put them into words. The signals are there, but the labels are missing, blurred, or delayed.

You might notice things like:

- Your heart is pounding, your chest is tight, but if someone asks "What are you feeling?" your brain offers, "Hungry?"
- You are clearly activated, but the only words you can reach for are "fine" or "tired."
- The emotional reaction shows up in your body before it ever makes sense in your mind.

So when something intense happens, your body might:

- Laugh
- Go very blank
- Get super chatty
- Change the subject suddenly

Not because you are trying to be fake, but because your brain hasn't caught up enough to say, “Oh, I'm scared and sad right now.”

If you grew up having to keep the peace, handle crises, or be “the strong one,” alexithymia can get even stronger. You learn to scan other people’s feelings faster than your own. Your system priority is “manage the room,” not “check in with myself.”

If you're neurotypical, the translation is: Imagine your emotional dashboard is in a language you sort of recognize, but you can't read fast enough in real time. By the time you understand “oh, that was grief,” the moment has already moved on.

So instead, the body does quick, confusing things like laugh and then freeze.

None of that means you are heartless. It means your wiring for noticing and naming feelings is different, and often running behind schedule.

Love, sadness, and the invisible hurt

Here is the painful joke of all this.

On the inside, many neurodivergent people feel very strong emotions, often more intense than the people around them. Care is high. Sensitivity is high. The volume knob is stuck on “max.”

On the outside, what people see is:

- Jokes at serious times
- Flat affect
- “Detached” storytelling about painful stuff
- Silence, shutdown, or changing the topic

That mismatch can be brutal. You might:

- Worry that you're secretly a bad person
- Replay conversations and cringe at how you sounded
- Feel hurt when someone assumes you don't care, when actually you're still thinking about it days later

A lot of the real hurt is invisible. It happens after the moment when the feelings finally land, and you're alone with them. That is when the tears come. Or the shutdown. Or the hours of scrolling because you can't bear to sit still with it.

If you're neurotypical, the translation is: Please do not use "how upset they look in the moment" as your only measure of how much something matters to them. The storm may arrive late, and it may happen out of sight.

Your friend who laughs when you tell them something scary might go home and not sleep for three nights. Their love for you is not measured by how much they resemble a movie reaction in the first five minutes.

How to support us (including yourself)

So what do you do with all this, besides replay old weird laughs at 2 a.m.?

For neurodivergent readers: First, drop the "I am broken" story a little bit. Your reactions make sense in context. They kept you safe enough to get here. You can start gently updating your settings without trying to rip out the wiring.

A few small shifts:

- When you notice you laughed at a heavy moment, you can name it out loud: "That laugh was my nerves, by the way. I do care." You don't have to give a full TED talk. Just a small translator note.

- When you feel that "wrong" reaction start, you can buy yourself time: "My brain is catching up. Can I text you about this after I sit with it a bit?" This lets people know something is happening, even if they can't see it yet.

- Privately, you can practice labeling slower: notice your body, then ask, "If this had a feeling name, what might it be?" You don't have to be right. You are just building a bridge between sensations and words. As an additional tip, you can revisit the chapter on feelings wheels in case that tool is helpful.

Selective sharing is allowed. You don't have to open your chest to everyone. You are allowed to be choosy about who gets the unarmored version.

Selective caring is not selfish. It is strategy.

For neurotypical readers: If someone in your life often "laughs at the wrong time," try holding this in mind: this might be their shield, not their verdict.

You can support them by:

- Taking them at their word, not just their facial expression. If they say, "I'm taking this seriously," believe that, even if they're also doing an awkward smile.

- Offering low-pressure follow-up. For example: "If your feelings about this land later, I'm still here." That signals you don't need the "right" reaction on your timeline.

- Asking curious, not accusing, questions. Instead of "Why are you laughing?" try "I noticed you laughed just

> now. Is that a nervous thing for you?" Only if you have that kind of trust, of course.

The goal is not to "fix" their reactions so they look more normal. The goal is to ensure enough safety that the armor can soften over time, if it wants to.

A small reframe to take with you

If you only remember one thing from this chapter, let it be this: That weird laugh, that flat voice, that off-timed joke, they're often signs of a system that is overwhelmed, not a heart that is empty.

You are allowed to care in delayed, sideways, messy ways. You are allowed to protect yourself while you do.

Laughing at the wrong time doesn't mean you're wrong. It just means your brain picked survival first, feelings second.

We can work with that.

You are not going to leave this chapter suddenly "good at feelings." What you are leaving with is language for two things that have probably been running in the background for years. Alexithymia, feelings with the labels rubbed off. And emotional armor, the jokes and chill and competence you wear so no one sees the mess underneath.

In the next chapters, when we talk about work, burnout, and being "the reliable one," you will see this armor show up again in office clothes. When we talk about caring in a world on fire, you will see alexithymia there too, in how hard it can be to tell whether you are actually numb or just overloaded.

Now that we can translate these signals, let us look at where those translations bump up against status and work life.

How To Watch Successful People Absolutely Botch Reality

By the time you hit this chapter, you have already spent some time inside your own emotional translation system. You have named things like alexithymia, emotional armor, and the way your brain tracks patterns other people don't even see. All of that comes with you to work, whether you want it to or not.

You know that feeling when you're sitting in a meeting, watching some very impressive person say something that is obviously wrong or half-baked, and your brain quietly whispers: "I am sorry, you what?"

On paper, they are a success story. Title, salary, LinkedIn glow, network full of "friends" who would absolutely sell them for stock options.

Inside your head, you're thinking, "I could see this train wreck six slides ago. Why am I not the person getting paid for this level of perception?"

We are going to use that perception without letting it poison you. Written by one of the people who can see the whole game board, and is still somehow stuck playing on the cheap seats.

This is the part you're not supposed to say out loud: Sometimes, you quietly believe you are better than the people winning.

Not better as a human. Better at reading people. Better at seeing risk. Better at guessing how this all turns out in six months. And yet, they get the money and the status. You get a front-row seat to the nonsense, a decent sense of existential rage, and maybe a migraine.

Let's talk about that. Honestly.

The quiet superiority you are not supposed to have

You are the one who can tell, five minutes into a meeting, who actually runs the place, who's pretending, and who's mentally checked out.

You clock the micro-expressions. The weird tone change. The way two people never speak directly, only through a slide deck. You can feel the politics move like weather.

So when some high-status person misses something that feels painfully obvious, your body reacts.

A little spike of disbelief. A tiny inner voice that says, "How did you not see that?" Maybe even, "If this is what counts as 'leadership,' I am a god."

It's not that you think you have no flaws. You know you're a mess. You probably have a very detailed list. You know you forget basic tasks, or freeze on simple emails, or lose whole afternoons to brain static. You know you're not a productivity robot.

But that is part of what makes this spicy. You are not comparing your best to their worst. You are comparing your everyday perception to their professional role, and still thinking, "Really? This is the bar?" That edge, that "I'm kind of better at this part," is not just ego. It is data.

Pattern recognition as a superpower (with no user manual)

Your brain is a pattern engine. It spots dynamics and risks that other people glide past.

You watch one interaction, and your system builds a whole predictive model. "That person is checked out. That one is scared of conflict. Those two are in a quiet power struggle. That project is dead in three months."

And you're usually not guessing. You are running thousands of tiny data points at speed. Tone, timing, word choice, who looked at whom, who stayed silent.

You can tell which value is real and which is just printed on a mug. You can tell which leader is actually kind and which one is performing "supportive boss" like a stage play.

Inside, you are thinking, "If you all listened to what I can see, we would save so much time and money."

You're probably right.

The problem is not that your perception is wrong. The problem is that perception is not the same currency as what success culture is actually trading.

You are fluent in reality. They are fluent in optics.

You think, "If I can see the truth, that should count." The system thinks, "If I can sell the story, that is what counts."

You are not broken. You're just not playing the same game.

Why the idiots are winning

Here is the rude part.

The people you are quietly calling “idiots” are often very good at things that your nervous system either hates or refuses to do without a fight.

They are willing to:

- Say things with more confidence than accuracy
- Play along with fake relationships and surface-level charm
- Treat work like a stage and themselves like the main character

You, on the other hand, are trying to say things you actually believe. You want a real connection, not networking as a sport. Your body revolts when you try to sell a story that your pattern recognition has already flagged as nonsense.

So they look bold.

You look “uncertain” or “quiet.”

They enter rooms already assuming they belong there. They don't seem to care if their idea is half-baked, because their brain doesn't ring a loud alarm about all the possible outcomes.

Your brain does.

Your brain is doing a full risk assessment in the background. It's running, “If I say this, who will get tense, what politics could that trigger, what if I am missing a piece, what does this commit me to, how do I protect myself if this goes badly?”

Of course it's harder to jump in with hot takes when your inner system is doing that kind of live calculation.

This is not stupidity on their side and pure genius on yours. It is different tolerances.

They tolerate being wrong in public much more easily than you tolerate feeling unsafe or out of integrity. They accept a level of self-mythology that makes your skin crawl.

So the world reads them as confident leaders and reads you as "smart, but not quite ready." It's not a fair reading. It's just the one the system is biased to make.

The pain of seeing it and not being paid for it

You're not mad that they exist. You are mad at the gap.

The gap between what you can see and what you can actually act on. The gap between how much value your perception creates and how much you get paid. The gap between their loud, messy success and your quiet, careful survival.

It can be brutal to watch people collect rewards for work that, from your perspective, is half insight and half theatre, while you're thinking: "I don't need millions. I just want some money that doesn't feel like bloodsport, and a few actually good people in my life."

You're not asking to be the next startup unicorn. You want your clarity to be worth something. You want your refusal to lie to yourself not to be punished.

You want friendship, not networking. Colleagues who are not smiling at you while mentally calculating your usefulness. You want less fake and more real.

You are not greedy. You are starving.

Naming the fantasy you're using against yourself

Part of why this hurts so much is the fantasy running in the background. The fantasy goes something like: "If I am really this perceptive, I should be as successful as they are, but ethically and with better taste in friends."

So every time you meet some high-status train wreck, part of you whispers, "If they can do it, what is wrong with me?"

You quietly turn their mess into your personal failure.

What if the actual fantasy is off?

What if your brain is not built for "big shiny success at all costs." What if it's built as a truth detector, a safety system, a meaning filter.

You are not failing.

You are just using the wrong fantasy as a measuring stick.

You are measuring yourself against people who are playing a completely different game, with completely different inner rules.

It is like comparing a thermometer to a fire extinguisher. They both show up around heat, but they're not trying to do the same job.

Let yourself be right (without making it your job)

Here is a small, slightly evil permission slip.

You are allowed to notice that someone is a successful idiot.

You are allowed to think, "Wow, you are very good at pretending this is fine." You are allowed to privately acknowledge, "I see more than you. I feel more than you. I care more than you."

That is not cruelty. That is accurate self-respect.

What you do not have to do is turn that perception into a new obligation. You do not have to be the secret conscience of the company. You do not have to rescue every doomed project. You do not have to "fix" leadership by writing the perfect feedback email that your nervous system is too smart to send.

You can let your pattern recognition be information, not a cursed leadership calling.

You can say, "I see this. It is real. And I am allowed to choose where I spend this level of sight."

Redefining what winning looks like for you

If you wait for the world to pay you exactly what your perception is worth, you will go quietly mad.

So let us cheat a little.

Instead of asking, "Why am I not as successful as these people?" try, "What kind of small, real success actually fits the brain I have?"

Maybe it's enough money that your nervous system can finally unclench. Work that does not constantly insult your intelligence. A tiny circle of people who are not lying to themselves all day.

That is not "aiming low." That is aiming true.

You can still be ambitious. You're just allowed to be ambitious about safety, integrity, and good company, instead of pretending you want the same trophy that makes other people feel important.

Your field guide does not have to end with you becoming the most ethical CEO alive. It can end with you having:

- Enough money to make survival not a full-time job
- Enough honesty around you that your brain is not constantly screaming

- Enough self-respect to know that seeing the truth is already a kind of wealth

You may never want the life of the successful idiot. That is fine.

You are building something more interesting. Something quieter. Something that actually feels like yours.

And if, along the way, you keep smirking in meetings because you can see exactly how this will go before everyone else catches up?

That is not a flaw. That is your amazing brain doing its job.

Redefining winning also means redefining what tools you need to do the work. In the next chapter, I will show how clothes and sensory context are not vanity but tools for doing your job well.

Why Your "Professional" Dress Code Hurts My Brain (And Work)

Picture the word consultant. You probably see a very specific person. Button-up shirt. Blazer. "Nice" shoes that hurt by lunch. Maybe a watch that costs more than my first car.

Now picture me. Still a consultant. Still doing the same level of work, thinking, and problem-solving. But in a hoodie. Soft shirt. Comfortable shoes. Maybe jeans, but only if it's really cold. Definitely not in the costume. From the outside, it can look like I am just refusing to "be professional." Like, I am trying to make a point. Or like I do not respect the client, the culture, or the job.

That is the moment this piece is for.

Because what you are not seeing in that outfit choice is sensory processing disorder. And once you understand that, the hoodie stops looking like a rebellion and starts looking like what it is. A tool that lets me actually do my job.

Sensory processing disorder is not "being picky"

Let us start with the basic thing: sensory processing disorder (SPD).

SPD means my brain and nervous system do not handle sensory input the way most people's do. Touch, sound, light, smell, even certain patterns. They don't just show up and wait for their turn. They grab the steering wheel.

For you, a stiff collar is "a bit annoying." For me, it can feel like a small, constant electric shock along my neck. You might notice the air conditioner buzzing. I might feel like it's drilling directly into my skull, every second that it runs.

From the outside, that difference is invisible. You see "shirt." I feel "attack."

This is why calling people with SPD "picky" or "dramatic" completely misses the point. I'm not chasing comfort the way some people chase luxury. I'm chasing basic functionality. If my clothes, the lights, the sounds, or the smells are wrong for me, my brain devotes so much energy to "survive this" that it has much less left for "do the work I am paid to do."

The irony is that I did not fully understand this before I became a consultant. I moved into a field with a strong visual stereotype, then realized later that standard "consultant drag" is exactly the kind of thing my nervous system hates most.

Surprise!

The clothing problem you can't see

Let's talk outfits, since that is where a lot of silent judgment lives. From your point of view, I have choices. I could put on the "proper" shirt, belt, shoes, and jacket. I could fit in. I could look like every other consultant that ever walked into a boardroom.

From my point of view, those are not simple choices. Each item is a sensor my brain has to fight.

A stiff collar means constant pressure on my neck. Seams in the wrong place mean my skin cannot stop yelling about it. A synthetic fabric that doesn't breathe means my body feels trapped. "Dress shoes" might have a texture, weight, or stiffness that makes every step part of a low-level panic.

And the key detail is this. It doesn't fade.

For many people, an annoying texture becomes background noise after a few minutes. For me, it often ramps up. The longer it's there, the louder my brain screams about it. While I'm trying to listen to a client, or present, or manage a delicate conversation, a different part of my brain is locked in a loop that sounds like: "Collar. COLLAR. COLLAR. COLLAR. COLLAR."

You don't see that. You just see a guy in a hoodie and think, "Weird hill to die on."

From my side, the hill is not fashion. It is access to my own focus.

Professionalism is not a costume

There is a quiet rule in many workplaces. Real professionals look a certain way. If you match the photo, people assume you are serious, capable, and trustworthy.

Here is the twist. If I try to look like the photo, I become less capable and less trustworthy, because I cannot do my best thinking while my body is screaming. I am a consultant who does not look like a consultant. And I'm okay with that.

Not because I want to be special. Not because I want to fight every culture norm on principle. But because my nervous system has limits, and if I pretend those limits are not real, you don't get my best work.

This is the part I really wish coworkers understood. When you see me in comfortable clothes, you're not seeing me "getting away with something." You're seeing the version of me that can:

- Listen closely without getting lost in sensory noise
- Think clearly instead of battling distraction from my own clothes
- Stay regulated, calm, and grounded in long meetings

In other words, you are seeing the most professional version of me, even if I don't look like the stock photo in the onboarding slide deck.

"Can you not just tolerate it?"

I know the thought that comes up. You might not say it out loud, but it is there. I get it, and I'm not offended by you having that thought.

"Can you not just tolerate it?"

Sometimes, yes. For a short time, at a high cost. I can mask, push through, and "act fine." A lot of autistic and SPD people have become very good at that. Here is the problem. There is always a bill. If I spend three hours in full sensory overload because I wanted to look "acceptable" to a client, I will pay for it. Maybe I crash after the meeting. Maybe I can't think clearly the rest of the day. Maybe I'm wiped out for the whole week.

That cost is invisible to you, but it's not imaginary. It means fewer good ideas, less energy for complex problems, fewer reserves for unexpected changes or crisis moments.

So when you see me choosing comfort first, I'm not choosing "easy" over "hard." I'm choosing sustainable over "melt down later in private."

Comfort is not a perk, it is an accommodation

Here is where the “slightly spicy PSA” part comes in.

We are very used to thinking about some accommodations as normal. Glasses. Standing desks. Ergonomic keyboards. Noise-canceling headphones, at least for “focus time.”

No one says, “If you were serious about this job, you would just stare at a blurry screen without glasses like the rest of us.” Yet when it comes to sensory needs that are less visible, like clothing, texture, or temperature, the default expectation is often, “Everyone else manages, so you should too.”

Comfort for me is not a perk. It is an accommodation. It is a way to reduce unnecessary sensory load so I can use that energy on the actual job.

If you would not ask someone to walk around all day without their mobility aid to “look more professional,” then asking me to abandon the sensory supports that keep me functional is the same kind of problem. Different flavor, same basic recipe.

This isn't about special treatment. It's about appropriate treatment so that I can bring the skills you hired me for.

What you can do differently

If you work with someone like me, here are a few simple shifts that matter more than you might think.

First, take clothing and environment conversations seriously. If a colleague says, “These lights really bother me,” or “I can't focus in that kind of fabric,” treat that as real data, not a quirky preference. You don't have to fully understand it to respect it.

Second, expand your picture of “professional.” A person can be thoughtful, sharp, and highly effective while not matching the mental picture you grew up with. A hoodie can sit right next to a deep understanding of your business problem.

Third, connect accommodations to outcomes. When I'm comfortable, I perform better. I'm more present. I make fewer mistakes. I have more patience. You are not doing me a personal favor. You are investing in better results.

Finally, remember that you are not seeing the whole cost of "just push through it." If someone tells you a specific environment, outfit, or sensory setup is tough for them, believe that they are already managing far more than you see.

Inviting you to my "dark side"

I want you to join me in questioning the automatic rules about how serious people "should" look. I want you to see that a consultant in a hoodie is not unprofessional by default. They might be doing the hardest work in the room: building a world where they can function as their real self, not as a costumed version that everyone else finds easier to recognize.

You don't have to fully feel what I feel to accept that SPD is real and that comfort is not optional for me. You only have to believe that I am telling you the truth about my own body.

If you can do that, suddenly the hoodie is not a problem to fix. It is just one more way a human nervous system has found to live and work in a world that was not really built for it.

And if that human happens to be the consultant you hired, the one in the comfortable shoes and the wrong jacket, you might find that letting them come as they are is the most productive decision you make all year.

By the time you get to this part of the book, we have spent a little while at work together. We have watched "successful idiots" botch reality in meetings, and we have walked through what it costs your nervous system to wear the right costume in order to be taken seriously. We have basically done a mini arc on what professionalism looks like when your brain and body do not fit the default template.

How To Care In A World On Fire (Without Melting Down)

Let's zoom out.

This is not just about workplaces, expectations, or social rules. It's about living on a planet that is sprinting through multiple crises at once, while your brain is built to notice everything.

Your sensitive, overworked nervous system picks up tiny tone shifts in meetings. It also absorbs every headline, siren, urgent post, and "you need to see this" text. No wonder you wake up already tired.

You know that feeling when your brain is juggling a dozen worries before you even find your glasses? Climate headlines. Political updates. A friend's spiral in a group chat. Your inbox. That one unanswered text from months ago that still shows up like a ghost. Your body is already braced for impact and you haven't even opened the news.

By the end of this chapter, you will have a simple way to choose what you respond to, what you mute, and how to recover after you care.

Because caring is not the problem.

Trying to care about everything, all the time, at full intensity is the problem.

Your nervous system is not failing; it is full

If you grew up autistic, had ADHD, or were otherwise neurodivergent, you may have been called "mature" or "an old soul." Translation: you learned to track everyone else's feelings like weather reports, and ignore your own forecast completely.

Fast forward a few decades. Now you have a brain with years of practice scanning for threats and suffering. And the world is, objectively, a lot. Of course you feel like you're always braced for impact.

There's nothing wrong with your empathy.

What is struggling is your nervous system capacity.

Think of your care like "slots" in a backpack. You can only load so much before the straps dig in and something snaps. You might have slots for family, work, relationships, health, money, and the state of the world.

Neurotypical people often have fewer open slots at once, or they can close some without guilt. Many neurodivergent people cannot. You notice more context, more injustice, more micro-signals. Your brain tries to respond to all of it like it's equally urgent.

That sounds noble. It also quietly destroys your ability to function.

Chronic over-caring can look like:

- Feeling guilty for resting, enjoying anything, or saying "I don't have the capacity right now."
- Doomscrolling until your shoulders hurt, then still feeling behind on information.

- Swinging between “I must fix everything” and “I can't even answer an email, what's the point?”

None of this means your values are wrong.

It means your settings got locked on: Maximum Sensitivity. No Off Switch Provided.

We're going to add some switches.

Selective caring is not selfish; it's strategy

There is a common idea that if you care about justice, you should care about everything equally, all the time.

That's not morality. That's math that doesn't work. Your body still needs sleep, food, and quiet. You get one human nervous system, not an unlimited subscription.

Also, your brain is already working overtime on:

- Sensory overload
- Social rules that often don't make sense
- Executive function puzzles like “how many days has that laundry been there?”

Then you tried to carry every crisis like a personal to-do list. No wonder your brain keeps hitting the “NOPE” button.

Here is the reframe: Selective caring is not you becoming cold. It is you becoming effective.

It's saying, “I will spend my limited care where it matters most, not where the algorithm points my face.”

That might look like:

- For politics, you choose one trusted newsletter or one solid weekly recap, not three platforms and thirty hot takes per day.
- You choose one or two causes that match your values and your skills, and you give those your real energy.
- Everything else gets witnessed, honored, and released, instead of adopted as your personal emergency.

You are not leaving the struggle.

You are picking your post.

Humor as a life jacket (not denial)

If you've masked for years, you already know how to joke through pain. You learned to turn your meltdown into a bit and your burnout into a punchline. Some of that humor kept you alive. Some of it kept people from seeing that you were drowning.

I'm not here to take humor away from you. I'm here to hand it back as a tool instead of a shield.

There is a difference between:

- "Nothing matters, let's laugh while the ship sinks."
- "Things matter so much that my brain needs a release valve so the lid doesn't blow off."

The first one numbs you. The second one helps you regulate so you can keep going.

You can still say, "Cool, my executive dysfunction has joined forces with the entire system, what a crossover episode," and then go take your meds, pay your bill, or email your insurance rep.

The joke doesn't cancel the action. Both can live in the same person.

How caring too much turns into freeze

Let’s name the pattern, because once you see it, it's hard to unsee.

You care a lot. So you try to stay informed. That means constant input. Your brain absorbs story after story until your body is buzzing like a live wire. Your thoughts speed up. Your attention gets jumpy. Soon, your options feel like:

- Fix everything
- Curl into a ball

Humans are not built for “fix everything,” so your nervous system chooses option three.

Freeze.

Freeze looks like:

- You scroll, but you're not really present.
- You want to act, but every action feels too small or too complicated, so you do none.
- You check out into shows, games, snacks, or loops that numb without truly restoring.

From the outside, it can look like apathy. Inside, it feels like being trapped behind glass, watching yourself not move.

That trapped feeling is not a moral failure. It is a nervous system that has spent years at capacity and finally blew a fuse.

The goal is not to "care less" as in "shrug at injustice." The goal is to turn down the background alarm so your caring can actually reach your hands, your schedule, and your choices.

Build a smaller, kinder news window

You don't need to know everything. You really, truly don't.

Your brain will insist you do because it confuses consuming information with taking responsibility.

Those are not the same thing.

Try a news window instead of a firehose. You decide how big the window is, when you open it, and when you close it. That is not ignorance. That is hygiene.

Ideas to try:

- Pick specific times to check heavy topics, and a firm stop time. "No doomstuff after 8 pm" is not dramatic. It is sleep protection.
- Choose one or two trusted sources that give you signals, not noise.
- When you feel the buzzed, shaky, jaw-tight "I'm suddenly cold" feeling, treat it like a fire alarm. Not a vibe. Exit the building. Close the apps. Put the phone in another room if you can.

You are not required to be an open window for the world's pain every second of the day.

You are allowed to check back in tomorrow from a rested brain and still be a caring person.

Choose your lane on purpose

You cannot care about everything at level 10 and also function as a single human organism. Your body has been trying to tell you that with migraines, shutdowns, insomnia, "weird" symptoms, and the permanent knot in your shoulders.

So here's the experiment: Instead of caring about everything at 3 percent effectiveness, what if you chose a few things to care about at 60 percent, with actual follow-through?

Choosing your lane is not a betrayal of other causes. It is a division of labor. It is trusting that other people are holding other pieces.

Your lane might be:

- Supporting one mutual aid group with time or money
- Being the person who can find accurate info on one specific topic
- Using your special interest, writing, art, spreadsheets, or organizing brain to support people already doing the work

You don't have to invent everything yourself. You don't have to be the face of anything. Quiet, consistent effort still counts.

When your brain tries to drag you back into "but what about literally every other horror," you can tell it: "I see that. I care. My role is here."

Then you come back to the thing you chose.

That is not apathy. That is boundaries.

Exhaustion dressed as ambition

Here is where things get extra sneaky.

A lot of neurodivergent people don't just over-care. We also over-prove.

Your brain starts to treat caring like a performance review. "If I just do more, I will finally feel okay. If I read more, share more, give more, show up more, I will finally be allowed to rest."

So you stack it up. Extra learning. Extra emotional labor. Extra "staying informed." Extra being the person who always knows what to say.

From the outside, it looks like competence. Inside, it feels like outrunning a quiet accusation: "Not enough. Never enough."

This is a brutal trap because the finish line is infinite. There is always another crisis. Another post. Another urgent update. Another way to feel behind.

You can't win a game that refreshes every ten seconds.

Protect the part of you that still wants a future

Under the exhaustion and numbness, there is a small, stubborn part of you that still imagines a future. Not perfect. Just livable.

A future where you're not constantly on the verge of collapse. Where you can enjoy a cup of coffee without guilt. Where you choose to help instead of feeling yanked around by every notification.

That part of you deserves protection.

Protecting it looks less glamorous than constant outrage. It looks like:

- Going to bed when you're tired, even if there is "more to read."

- Eating before you scroll heavy topics, so your body isn't running on adrenaline
- Letting yourself enjoy softness, joy, and silliness without attaching a guilt footnote

You are not weak for needing those things. You are a mammal. Mammals need rest and warmth and connection, or they lose it.

You will not save the world by white-knuckling your way through another year of burnout. You might help build something better by lasting long enough to keep showing up.

Caring, but not constantly

You're allowed to keep your tender, outraged, hopeful heart. You don't have to become detached to survive.

You're also allowed to stop offering your nervous system as a 24/7 sacrifice to every headline.

You can care intentionally instead of constantly. You can be informed without being consumed. You can pick a lane without abandoning your values.

You are not broken for needing limits. You are learning a skill most of us were never taught: How to stay human in a world that profits from you burning out.

That tired, caring, slightly crispy version of you on the couch right now?

Worth protecting.

In the next chapter, we'll look at how your brain turns a long day of caring into a long night of vigilance.

Tiny Trailer, Big Rest: What My Neurodivergent Brain Taught Me About Sleep

You know that feeling when your body is lying in bed, but your brain has already clocked in for the night shift?

Like your head hits the pillow and suddenly there's a full staff meeting, a security briefing, a highlight reel of everything you ever said in eighth grade, and a very detailed slideshow about global collapse.

Welcome to sleep as unpaid labor.

This is for you if you have a neurodivergent brain, or a very suspicious brain that thinks it might be neurodivergent, and you are so, so tired of being tired. It's not that you hate sleep. It's that sleep feels like a job you keep failing at, in a body and a world that don't feel set up for you.

We're going to poke at why your brain treats night like a work shift, and then change the actual conditions around your sleep so your system can stand down a little. Not to some perfect, influencer-level sleep routine. Just to "I don't start the day already in the red."

You are not lazy. You are under-rested.

And a lot of that is because your brain thinks it is on security duty.

Your security-guard brain

Imagine your brain as a very serious security guard.

Neon vest. Walkie-talkie. Too much coffee. Standing in the lobby of your life, muttering, "Absolutely not, we are not taking our eyes off this."

That is your nervous system.

Earlier, we talked about your capacity like an overachieving smoke alarm, blaring for every bit of heat in the room. This security guard is the same system from a different angle, the part of your brain that tries to answer every crisis tab all day and then refuses to clock out at night.

If you grew up in tight spaces, chaotic spaces, or "always on alert" spaces, your guard got promoted early. If you're autistic, ADHD, sensory sensitive, or some mix of "this world was not designed for me," that guard has probably never gotten to clock out.

So you lie down in bed. Your body thinks, "Rest time." Your security-guard brain thinks, "Perfect. We can finally do our rounds with no distractions."

That is why you get the late-night brain parade:

- The replay of every awkward interaction
- The mental to-do list that somehow includes tasks from 2009
- The imaginary arguments
- The scrolling "state of the world" report

You're not broken. Your guard is just overtrained.

It learned that sleeping deeply in the wrong place, at the wrong time, in the wrong environment, was unsafe. So now it treats "going to sleep" like "walking away from the control panel while everything is on fire."

This is why "just relax" does nothing.

You are not bad at relaxing. Your brain simply does not believe the building is safe enough for the guard to sit down.

Why your brain trusted the tiny trailer

For a while over the summer, my wife and I lived in a tiny travel trailer.

By every Pinterest standard, this should have been a sleep disaster. Cramped space. Limited storage. Everything close together. No minimalist neutral bedroom with soft linen and one tasteful plant.

And yet.

My brain slept better there.

Because the trailer sent a very specific message to my nervous system: I can see the whole space at once.

There were no mysterious noises from ten rooms away, albeit some locations had even more mysterious sounds coming from somewhere outside. No echoey hallway for your brain to patrol. No "what was that creak" from a distant wall. My security guard could look around, see every corner in a single glance, and go, "Alright. I've got eyes on everything. We can power down a little."

It was not "perfect sleep hygiene." It was perceived safety.

When we got back home and moved into a bigger house, with more space and more doors and more surfaces and more everything, my brain quietly went back on high alert. More unknowns. More places for sound to bounce. More work for the guard.

To everyone else, I "upgraded," but to my nervous system, I expanded the perimeter and fired half the staff.

So when people say, "Your bedroom is so nice, you must sleep great," and I'm thinking, "I have never been more exhausted," that is why. The decor is fine. The felt safety is not.

My brain isn't dramatic. It is loyal.

It will stay up until 3 a.m. walking circles in that bigger space, just to keep me alive.

When rest doesn't rest: post-COVID fog

Then there is the kind of tired that sleep doesn't touch.

After COVID, a lot of brains like ours met a new level of fog. You could sleep. You could nap. You could lie there for twelve hours. And still wake up feeling like someone filled your head with wet cardboard.

This is not "I stayed up too late." This is "my whole operating system is running through molasses."

You forget words mid-sentence. You open a tab and have no idea why. You start a simple task and your brain just… idles. The security guard is there, but even they are leaning on the wall, squinting at the cameras, trying to stay vertical.

That fog feeds right back into the night.

Because if your brain spends the entire day working twice as hard to track basic things, it hits the pillow thinking, "We didn't keep up. We're behind. We have so much to fix." The guard pulls an extra shift, trying to replay, reorganize, make sense of it all. Which, of course, makes the fog worse the next day.

You're not imagining it. It really is harder for your system to do the same things it used to do.

And if you are neurodivergent on top of that, you were already running a more complex setup. Your brain has extra adapters, fine-tuning knobs, and emergency workarounds. COVID fatigue walks in, yanks a few cables, and walks away. No wonder your dashboard lights up.

This is important: if sleep feels like work and waking up also feels like work, that is not a moral failure.

That is your body and brain trying to reboot in a storm.

Your bedroom is a workplace, not a spa

Let's talk about your bedroom like it's a workplace, because for your security-guard brain, it is. If you walk into a job site where:

- The lights are wrong for your eyes
- The noise level is unpredictable
- The furniture doesn't fit your body
- The temperature is never quite right

You don't relax. You brace.

A lot of "grown-up" bedrooms are built to impress visitors more than to calm actual brains. Big open spaces. High ceilings. Echoes. Decor instead of function. Nightstands that look nice but don't hold what you actually need when you wake up at 3 a.m.

If you've ever slept better on a couch, in a car, or in that tiny trailer than in your Official Bedroom, that is your nervous system voting.

Small, enclosed, "den" style spaces often feel more secure to sensitive brains. Less to scan. Fewer variables. Closer walls that give your body a sense of containment.

Your brain doesn't care if the room looks like an Instagram mood board. It cares whether it can stand down.

So instead of asking, "Is my bedroom nice?", try, "Would my overcaffeinated internal security guard feel safe taking a nap in here?"

Very different question. Very different answers.

Making sleep less like a shift you hate

We're not going to fix capitalism, long COVID, and sensory overload in one chapter, nor do I have the power to do so.

What we can do is change a few conditions so your security-guard brain has a shot at resting. Think of these as small union wins for your nervous system.

You don't have to do all of them. You aren't building the ultimate sleep temple. You're just making it less of a job to lie down.

1. Shrink the space your brain has to watch.

If big rooms keep you wired, give yourself a smaller "pod" inside the room.

That might look like:

- Pulling the bed into a corner instead of the middle, so you have walls on at least two sides.
- Using a curtain, canopy, or even a sheet to create a more enclosed sleep zone.

- Storing visual clutter out of your immediate sightline so your brain isn't inventorying piles every night.

You're not regressing by wanting smaller. You're recreating the feeling your brain prefers in a smaller space: I can see it all. It is contained. I can rest.

2. Give your guard an off-duty signal.

Your nervous system doesn't understand "should." It understands signals.

If scrolling in bed tells your brain "we are still gathering intel," it won't shut down. If you want to keep your phone nearby for safety or executive function, fine. Just add one clear, repeatable action that means, "We're off the clock now."

Maybe it's:

- Turning on one specific lamp and turning the overhead light off.
- Switching to a particular playlist you only use at night.
- Doing the same three-minute stretch on your bed every time you are actually trying to sleep.

The point is not perfection. The point is pattern. Your brain loves patterns. After enough repeats, that tiny ritual becomes a cue: "Guard can sit. Cameras still rolling, but no active patrol."

3. Make the room friendlier to your actual senses.

If you're neurodivergent, your sensory profile is not "average." So "normal bedroom" rules might be working against you.

- If silence makes your brain louder, allow a sound blanket, like consistent fan noise, rain sounds, or a boring podcast you don't care about.

- If the dark stresses you out, use the kind of low light that feels comforting instead of spooky. Nightlights are not childish. They are functional.
- If certain textures make your skin crawl, stop punishing yourself with them just because they were on sale or "look nice." Your body will not relax on a battlefield of Wrong Fabrics.

This is not "being picky." This is accessibility for your nervous system.

4. Let your dog be emotional infrastructure.

If you have a Seymour in your life, you already know.

Animals, especially the ones who have basically grafted themselves onto your soul, are regulation devices. A dog asleep at your feet, pressed against your legs, or even snoring in the same room, tells your security-guard brain something simple: "If there was real danger, they wouldn't be like this."

Your brain trusts your dog's body in a way it might not trust your own stories about "everything is fine."

That isn't silly. That is smart.

So if Seymour's dream-barking is what lets your system soften, that is not a quirk. That is assistive technology. You are allowed to design sleep around that.

You are not failing at rest

If sleep feels like work, it's not because you're doing rest wrong. It's because:

- Your brain was trained to stay on watch.

- Your environment sends “unsafe” signals your body actually believes.
- Illness and exhaustion have dragged you past the point where “a good night’s sleep” fixes anything in one shot.

You are navigating all of that with a brain that is already wired differently. Of course you feel like you're always behind.

So instead of trying to force yourself into someone else’s idea of rest, start from the most basic question: What would make my security-guard brain feel 5 percent safer here?

Not perfect. Not cured. Just a tiny bit less on duty. That's a valid goal. That is rest, too. You are not lazy. You are a tired, overworked brain in a big, noisy world, trying to keep you alive.

Make the job easier, and sleep starts to feel a little less like work. And when sleep stops being a shift you fail at, you will have more capacity to practice the small no's that preserve your day.

I Don't Wanna: A Field Guide for Grown-Up No's

There is a very specific kind of tension that shows up on date night.

You're out with your partner. You love them. You like being with them. You've already used a lot of words and made a lot of eye contact. You're starting to feel that quiet, rising overwhelm that doesn't quite have a name. They lean in and say, "Do you want to stay for another drink?" or "Do you want to see this movie?"

You scan yourself.

And what you find is not a clear reason. What you find is one clean, stubborn feeling.

I just don't want to.

No big story. No tidy explanation. Just a full body no. In this chapter, we'll build a simple translation script and a capacity check so you can say no without a courtroom-level explanation.

It's mostly for the neurodivergent person who lives there frequently. The autistic or ADHD or otherwise "spiky profile" brain that gets full before the world expects it to. It's also, a bit, for the neurotypical partner who's watching our faces and thinking, “You don't want to? Like, at all? What did I do?”

Let's pull this apart together.

What “I just don’t want to” usually means (for neurodivergent brains)

From the outside, “I just don't want to” can look lazy, selfish, or childish. Like you're refusing to compromise or be spontaneous. Inside, it is almost never about willpower. It's about capacity.

By the time you're in that date-night moment, your brain has usually been juggling a lot of hidden tasks. You've tracked sounds, lights, people, social rules. You've remembered what your face is doing. You've pushed yourself through small talk or schedule changes that are only “no big deal” for people whose nervous systems are not already living at a 7 out of 10.

When I say capacity here, I mean the same thing we talked about in the “capacity myth” section. Your brain isn't a bottomless well. You get a limited number of care slots and energy units for the day, and once they're spent, they are spent, no matter how good the plan looks on paper. That tired “I just don't want to” is usually your nervous system filing a quiet report that says, “We're out of bandwidth, not out of love.”

So when your partner says, “Do you want to stay longer?” what they hear as a small ask lands in your body as: Do you want to push yourself past your current limit, on purpose, with no clear exit plan?

And your whole system goes, "Absolutely not, thank you for coming to my TED Talk." That is the “I just don’t want to.” It's not random. It's the surface signal of things like:

- Social exhaustion. Your conversation fuel is empty, even if you're still being polite.

- Sensory overload. The bar, the movie theater, the crowd is already too loud, too bright, too much.
- Task switching cost. Shifting from "I thought we were going home" to "actually, new plan" is not a light pivot. It's a heavy lift.

You might not have words for any of that in the moment. All you have is the result: an unmovable no.

Why it is so hard to explain

Here's the double bind that many of us live in.

On the one hand, partners say, "Just tell me what's going on. Communicate." That sounds reasonable. On the other hand, what's going on is often: "I'm tracking forty micro-stimuli plus your mood plus whether my facial expression matches my words, while my brain screams that I'm maxed out but also terrified of disappointing you. I need to leave before I shut down or snap at you for asking one more normal question."

Which doesn't go very well over appetizers. So instead, we try to find "real" reasons. We reach for things that will sound valid to someone who does not feel what we feel. "I am tired." "I have a headache." "I need to get up early." Some of those might be true. Some might just be code for "My nervous system is cooked, and I cannot do more of this without burning myself."

The problem is, once you give a reason, people try to solve the reason.

You say, "I'm tired." They say, "We can leave in an hour, that way you still get sleep."

You say, "I don't like that kind of movie." They say, "What if we pick a different one?"

They are trying to help. But what you were actually saying, underneath, was not "Please fix the conditions." You were saying, My capacity is done. This is not a puzzle. This is a limit. When that gets missed, it feels like your "no" is being treated as a negotiation instead of a boundary. Which only makes you more drained and more dug in.

Dear neurodivergent reader: you are not broken for having a hard no

Let me talk to you directly for a second. That moment where you think, "I just don't want to, and I have no socially acceptable explanation"? That is usually your nervous system, not your morals. You're not selfish for having limits. You're not a bad partner because your bandwidth runs out sooner than theirs. Your internal "this is too much" meter is not a character flaw. It is a piece of safety equipment.

At the same time, it makes sense if you feel guilty or defensive. Many of us spent years being told: "Stop being difficult." "You are overreacting." "Everyone else is fine with this. Why aren't you?"

So now, when your partner gently asks to stay for one more drink, your body hears the ghost of every time someone demanded more than you had to give. Of course you tense up. Of course you brace for a fight. What helps is separating two truths inside yourself:

- Your limit is real. You don't owe your body more than it has.
- Your partner's disappointment is also real. They're allowed to want more time, more closeness, more fun.

Nobody is the villain in that math. There's just a mismatch in capacity and expectation. Your job is not to erase that mismatch. Your job is to describe it as clearly and kindly as you can, so both of you can work with reality instead of guessing.

Dear neurotypical partner: it is not about you (even when it affects you)

Now I'm looking at you, the partner who keeps hearing “I just don't want to” and feeling stung.

You're not imagining it. Your neurodivergent partner often wants less of certain things than you do. Less talking, less time out, fewer last-minute changes, fewer “come on, it will be fun” adventures. It can feel like rejection. Like if they loved you more, they would want what you want. That is a very human story. It's usually just the wrong story.

For many neurodivergent people, want is not a free-floating preference. It's chained to capacity. If their social and sensory load is already high, their “want” shrinks no matter who is asking. It's not a vote on you. It's a vote on “Can my brain and body do more of this without short-circuiting?”

You might not see the cost of staying longer at the bar or sitting through the movie they're not into. What you see is a person who can function, who can make small talk, who looks basically fine. What you do not see is the recovery bill that comes later. The shutdown the next day. The headache. The flat affect. The fact that they might have to cancel something else, or quietly fall apart, to pay for pushing past their limit for you.

When you respond to their “I don't want to” with, “Come on, just this once,” it doesn't make them feel loved. It makes them feel like their internal red alert is being dismissed because it's not visible to you.

If you want more closeness, one of the best gifts you can give is to believe their no the first time. Treat it as data, not a debate.

Translating "I don't want to" into something you can both use

So what do you do with all of this, in the actual moment?

This is where we get into translation, not performance. I'm not asking you to mask harder or become a saint. I'm inviting you to turn "I just don't want to" into language that shows the shape of what's going on. For the neurodivergent partner, that might look like:

- Swapping "I don't want to" for "I don't have capacity for that."
- Naming the type of drain, even briefly. "My social battery is empty." "My brain thought we were going home and it's stuck on that track."
- Adding care to the boundary. "I love you and I'm done for tonight. Can we plan something tomorrow when I have more in the tank?"

You're not required to give a full TED Talk on your neurology every time. Short is fine. The goal is to move from "I'm being difficult" or "You're being demanding" to "Our systems have different limits, so let us work with that."

For the neurotypical partner, translation might sound like:

- Asking capacity questions, not just preference questions. Instead of "Do you want to stay?", try "Do you have capacity to stay another hour, or are you done?"
- Showing you believe them. "If you're done, we can go. I would love more time, but I trust your limit."
- Moving the "more" you want into a different context. "I'm a little sad to leave, because I like being out with you. Maybe we can plan a quieter date this weekend?"

None of this fixes the fact that sometimes you will want different things. It does make those moments less like a secret war and more like a joint problem you're both facing.

When "I don't want to" is allowed to just be true

Underneath all the scripts and science, this comes down to something simple and kind of radical. You are allowed to not want something, even if someone you love really wants it. And they are allowed to feel disappointed, even while they respect your no.

That is it. That is the work.

If you're the neurodivergent partner, your growth edge might be letting yourself say, "I don't have capacity for that," before you hit the wall, and trusting that you're not ruining everything by having limits.

If you're the neurotypical partner, your growth edge might be letting that answer land, without turning it into a referendum on your worth, and staying curious about what would feel good for both of you.

Sometimes, date night will look like pushing a little, together, into something new. Other times, love will look like leaving the bar early, or skipping the movie, or going home when the invisible meter hits full. You don't need a better explanation than "I just don't want to" for your body to matter. You might, however, need better language so you and your partner can see what is already true.

You are not the problem. The mismatch is not the problem.

The silence around it is.

Once you both start naming what's actually happening, "I just don't want to" stops being a brick wall and starts being a doorway into the kind of relationship where everyone gets to be a person, limits and all.

Before we practice keeping those no's, it helps to know why your brain so often 'knows' the next move. Understanding prediction helps you trust your internal no and make it stick.

PREDICTIVE PROCESSING 2.0: WHY YOU ALWAYS KNOW WHAT COMES NEXT

I used to joke that I was kind of psychic.

Not in a crystal ball way. More in a "I can tell three months ahead of time which coworker is about to quit, which raid is about to wipe, and which group chat friendship is about to quietly fall apart" way. The same brain that acts like an overachieving smoke alarm, that will not sleep, that tries to answer every crisis tab, is also running predictions all the time about what might go wrong in the room.

I noticed patterns. I felt the mood of a room snap from relaxed to tense in half a second. I knew when someone was smiling with their mouth and panicking with their eyes.

People thought it was intuition. Or emotional intelligence. Or that I was just very perceptive. I thought so too, for a while.

Now I know: I am not psychic. My brain is just very, very loud.

And if you're reading this, there's a good chance yours is too and we'll talk about how to lower the volume on that prediction engine so it stops eating your energy.

When "psychic" is just pattern recognition on hard mode

Let me start with two familiar scenes.

At work, a new person joins the team. They say all the right things in meetings. They seem fine. Everyone else relaxes. But you don't.

You notice how they tense up when a certain manager speaks. The way they go quiet in planning calls. The way they start coming in five minutes late, then ten, then fifteen. You clock every micro-flinch around deadlines, every "oh, it's nothing" that is clearly not nothing.

You know, in your body, they're going to quit.

You can't prove it. You have no "evidence" that would hold up if you tried to bring it up. Still, your brain files it under "basically already true."

Then, a few months later, they hand in their notice. Everyone is shocked. But you're not.

Same thing in games.

You join a group. You're doing a raid, or some co-op thing, and on the surface everyone seems chill. Voice chat is full of jokes. People say it's "just for fun."

Except.

There is that one friend whose tone gets a little too sharp when someone messes up. The pause before they say "it's okay". The way the leader starts over-explaining mechanics to one specific person. Someone dies once, and there's this tiny shift in the air.

Your brain throws a flag.

You can tell, long before anyone quits the group or starts a fight, that this isn't going to be a team you stay with. The wipe that "comes out of nowhere" for everyone else feels like a replay to you. You already watched it in your head.

From the outside, it looks like magic. From the inside, it feels like drowning in data.

Your brain, the overcaffeinated pattern machine

Under all the jokes about being psychic, there's a very real thing your brain is doing. You are constantly taking in signals, then comparing them to patterns you've already seen.

Tiny changes in voice. Who interrupts who. What happens before someone storms off or disappears. How fast people reply. How someone laughs when they're relaxed, versus when they're not.

Your nervous system is running a prediction engine in the background: "This, plus this, plus this usually equals that."

If you're neurodivergent, that engine often runs hotter and faster. You notice more. You store more. You replay more. Your brain connects dots other people don't even see as dots.

So you end up with:

- A backlog of "I've seen this movie, I know how it ends" moments, and
- Almost no socially acceptable way to say "Hey, the vibes are off and my pattern recognition is screaming" without sounding rude, paranoid, or like you're accusing someone of something.

So you sit there, buzzing, holding information you can't use, and you call it being psychic.

It's not magic. It's pattern recognition mixed with hypervigilance.

And it's exhausting.

Reading the room vs being okay in the room

There's an idea that if you can read people well, you must be good with people. If you can sense tension, track feelings, and predict outcomes, that must mean you are socially skilled. That you are fine.

Often, the opposite is true.

Being good at reading the room is not the same as being okay in the room.

When your brain is this loud, every room can feel like an open browser with twenty tabs auto-playing. You are tracking:

- The person who is upset but pretending not to be
- The manager who is about to explode
- The friend who is getting left out of the conversation
- The joke that landed wrong but no one is addressing
- The future fight that hasn't yet started but is already building

You know where the tension is. You can map the social weather of the space with painful precision.

What you often cannot do is relax.

Your body treats "I know this is about to go badly" as if it's already happening. Your heart rate doesn't wait. Your muscles don't wait. Your brain doesn't say "ah yes, a prediction". It says, "We are in danger right now!"

So everyone else is still in the "ha ha, it's probably fine" phase, and you're already in the "post-crisis cleanup in aisle five" phase.

You're stuck bearing the full impact of something that technically hasn't happened yet.

That is not emotional intelligence. That is overload.

Why this "gift" wrecks your capacity

There's a reason this kind of knowing leaves you wiped out.

Every time you walk into a room, open a group chat, or log into a game, your brain spins up the simulation machine. It starts generating possible futures. Who might be hurt. Who might leave. What might break. It's trying to protect you. Or protect everyone. Or both.

You end up living the same conflict two or three times: Once when you feel it coming. Once when it actually happens. Sometimes again when you replay it later, checking your pattern library.

That is a lot of emotional labor for things you never chose.

It also messes with your decisions.

If you already know how something tends to go, you start opting out early. You leave groups before they fall apart. You distance yourself from coworkers who feel unstable. You drop out of games after the third small red flag, long before anyone else would say there's a problem.

From the outside, you can look flaky. Or pessimistic. Or like you, "never give things a chance."

From the inside, it feels like triage. Your nervous system is already maxed out. You don't have the spare capacity to sit around and wait to see if your prediction is wrong.

So you move. You quit. You bail.

And you carry the secret, quiet guilt that comes from always seeming too sensitive to things other people barely notice, while also being right so often it's almost worse.

You're not a broken crystal ball

If this is you, I want you to hear this clearly: You are not dramatic. You are not making it up. You are not "reading too much into things".

Your brain is doing a very advanced, very intense version of something all brains do. It's not a personal flaw. It's an unfiltered skill mixed with a nervous system that has been taught to stay on high alert. And like any unfiltered skill, it can hurt you.

Being right about people or situations is not the same as being safe with them. Being able to predict an outcome is not the same as being able to change it.

You are allowed to be proud of your pattern recognition and still admit that it's burning you out.

You can say: "I am good at seeing how things are going to go. I am also very tired, and my body pays a high price for carrying this much future in it all the time."

Both can be true.

Giving your loud brain some padding

You don't have to turn this part of you off. You probably couldn't if you tried.

What you can do, though, is give it more padding.

You can notice when your "I know how this ends" feeling switches on and treat it like a weather report rather than a prophecy. It is useful information, but it is not a command.

You can remind yourself:

- I am allowed to step back from situations that feel bad in my body, even if no one else sees it yet.
- I do not have to convince anyone I'm right. My nervous system doesn't need a courtroom. It needs care.
- Being early to the pattern doesn't mean I have to be the one to fix it, explain it, or hold it for everyone.

You aren't a warning siren for other people's lives. You don't have to stand in every burning building just because you smelled the smoke first.

So what does self-understanding look like?

For me, it looked like changing the story from "I'm weirdly psychic" to "I have a brain that is very loud and very fast at making sense of social patterns."

It looked like:

- Feeling less confused about why I was so tired after "nothing happened" at work or on a game night.
- Being kinder to myself when I bailed early from groups that felt off, instead of forcing myself to stay to prove I was patient.
- Naming the difference between reading the room and being okay in the room, and finally respecting that second part as an actual need, not a failure.

You don't have to celebrate every part of this. You don't have to love that your brain does it. But you can stop calling yourself broken. You can stop assuming everyone else sees what you see and just handles it better.

A lot of the time, they truly are not seeing it. You are.

You are not psychic. Your brain is just very loud. And now that you know that, you get to start building a life that makes room for the volume.

Now that you see why your brain is loud, let's imagine what happens when you give that brain a little care: a life with fewer reactive grabs and more chosen yeses. That is what the final chapter sketches.

Mask Off, Life On: A Small Future-You Montage

You made it.

You, with the overclocked brain and the tired eyes and the "I'll read one page and then nap forever" nervous system, somehow got all the way here.

That is not small. That is huge!

This whole book has basically been a long conversation about what happens when a high-sensitivity, high-care, deeply awake brain tries to survive in a world that runs on speed, denial, and pretending everything is fine. We named the patterns, we pulled at the loose threads of masking, we tried a few tiny switches instead of one giant life overhaul.

Now we're at the part where I get to look at you and say, "So... You did that."

An ordinary day, but easier to breathe in

Notice something important. Your life probably doesn't look magically different right now.

Same group chats. Same news cycle. Same people needing things. Same brain that can see twelve angles of harm in any situation and then still forget where it put its keys.

What's different is that you have more language, more levers, and a slightly kinder story about yourself.

Maybe you started one tiny thing while you read. A 3 pm reset alarm. A "do I actually have the capacity for this?" check-in before you say yes. A bit less performance in one relationship, even if it was only for five minutes.

That is enough to count.

One small change is worth choosing over "waiting for the perfect time" forever. One change can turn into two. Two can turn into "Oh, I kind of live differently now and didn't even send an announcement email."

You're not starting from scratch

There's a lie that says the hard part is changing your whole life.

For people like you, the hardest part was believing your experience mattered enough to even look at. To pick up a book like this. To keep reading even when your brain tried to spiral into "other people have it worse" or "what if I'm just being dramatic."

You already did the impossible part.

You noticed yourself. You stayed with your own discomfort long enough to get curious. You let yourself imagine a version of yourself whose not just a walking help desk in a human costume.

From here, everything else is repetition and practice. Not perfection, not a total personality transplant, just more reps with the new settings.

You already know how to do hard things. You've been doing hard things your entire life, mostly without a manual and usually while feeling like you were failing at the basics. This time you get to try them with a little more context and a lot less self-blame.

Tiny shifts, real futures

Here's what "success" might look like after this book, and I want you to notice how small it sounds on paper and how big it might feel in your actual body: You catch yourself mid-spiral at least once and think, "Ah. My nervous system is overloaded. That's data, not proof that I'm broken."

You pause before saying yes to a new thing and ask, "What will this cost Future Me?" Then you adjust something, even if the only thing you adjust is your expectations of yourself.

You have one conversation with someone in your life where you let your mask slip by about 10%. You don't give them your entire internal PowerPoint. You just tell the truth a tiny bit sooner.

Maybe you mention something you learned here. Maybe you say, "I read this book that made me feel less like an alien." Maybe that person feels a little less alone, too.

That is world-changing behavior wearing very ordinary clothes.

You, but with a little more room

You didn't read this to become a better machine. You read this because some quiet part of you wants more room. More room to care selectively. More room to rest without earning it. More room to be a whole person in a burning world, not just the one holding the fire extinguisher.

So take a second, right here at the end, and notice: there is already a bit more room around your edges. You know a few more exits.

You can see a light in the tunnel, and this time it doesn't feel like something that will disappear the second you reach for it.

You don't have to sprint toward it. You can walk. You can crawl. You can take six breaks and complain the whole way. The light will still be there, rolling its eyes fondly and waiting for you anyway.

Before you go

Consider this your little congratulations card from the future.

You made a choice to treat your own experience as something worth studying instead of something to crush into the shape that other people wanted. You practiced a different kind of honesty with yourself. You let hope in, even if it's only sitting in one corner of your chest for now.

That counts.

You are allowed to close this book and not immediately fix your entire life. You are allowed to just be a person who learned a few new things about how their brain and heart work, and to let those things spread on their own time.

We will call this “good enough for now” and let Future You take it from here.

I'm glad you made it this far, and I'm proud of how much further you will get, on your own timeline. I'll be over here doing the same work, taking off my own mask in small, real ways. You don't have to rip yours off all at once. You just have to keep giving your actual self a little more room to breathe.

www.ingramcontent.com/pod-product-compliance
Lightning Source LLC
LaVergne TN
LVHW100309210926
848480LV00003B/1065
* 9 7 9 8 9 9 4 3 7 3 1 0 1 *